BETWEEN SILENCE & SONG

WOMEN'S PRAYERS FOR ISRAEL'S DAYS
OF REMEMBRANCE & CELEBRATION

COMPILED & EDITED BY

SHIRA LANKIN SHEPS

RACHEL SHARANSKY DANZIGER

ANNE GORDON

AZ NASHIR: BETWEEN SILENCE & SONG
Women's Prayers for Israel's Days of Remembrance & Celebration

Book Cover Calligraphy by Malka Klein: www.malkaklein.com
Book Cover Design by Yitzchak Woolf
Typesetting by Yitzchak Woolf

Printed in Israel

ISBN: 979-8-218-63865-8

Dedication

This book is dedicated to the memories of those who perished in the Holocaust and to the lives lost in the defense and building of Israel. Their sacrifices form the bedrock of our history and are woven into the spirit of our nation.

We honor the resilience and bravery of our soldiers and their families, the unwavering spirit of Israel's many volunteers, and the steadfast love of the people across our land who, day by day, keep the heart of Israel alive. Their courage in the face of adversity lights our way and guards our future.

To the future of Israel: our children, our hope, and our tomorrow– we also dedicate this work. May they inherit a world of peace and fulfillment, and may they always hold on to the legacy of strength and faith that defines our people.

Through these prayers, we connect past, present, and future, weaving together the threads of memory, valor, and hope into the fabric of our shared journey.

Table of Contents

TEKES MA'AVAR
A Ceremony Marking the Transition from
Yom HaZikaron to Yom HaAtzmaut

YOM HAATZMAUT
Celebrating Israel's Independence and Statehood

LAG BAOMER
33rd Day of the Omer: Joy, Bonfires, and Tradition

YOM YERUSHALAYIM
Marking Jerusalem's Reunification in 1967

Foreword

Az Nashir was born out of a real need for language and comfort. So many of us struggled to give voice to our new realities in the post-October 7th world.

The first volume, *Az Nashir: We Will Sing Again*, was published in the fall of 2024, in the throes of war. Women all over Israel wrote prayers while rockets flew overhead, soldiers fell in battle, and families lived in cramped hotel rooms far away from home. The book went to print while wounded soldiers struggled to recover, hostage families cried out for their loved ones, and the families of our soldiers counted minutes with their husbands and wives, their sons and daughters. The book came into the world days before Israel's ground invasion of Lebanon and the new dangers and losses it incurred. The urgency was immense, the distress high, and a movement of women expressing their deepest prayers from the heart, and sharing them with a community, could not have been more timely.

At the time of our book launch, rockets were flying, many hostages were trapped in Gaza, families were separated by war. Hundreds of women came from all over Israel to Jerusalem to pray together, to sing, to recite *tefillot*, and to be inspired by the incredible art featured in the book. In the months following the launch, we traveled from community to community, bringing the prayers to new audiences who found solace in the words and art of our writers and artists, and joined our growing community. We facilitated workshops on the prayers, and encouraged women to write their own *tefillot*, too.

We have heard from thousands of women, in Israel and all over the world, who have been nourished by our first volume. It has unlocked many words of prayer that might have otherwise gone unspoken, opened channels of communication with the Divine, as well as with people who felt blocked by trauma and grief, and brought together a prayerful movement that has been deeply personal, powerful, and transformative.

The book in your hands, *Az Nashir: Between Silence & Song*, grew out of more months of ongoing war, additional losses, and a prevailing sentiment of determination to live Jewishly in our land, despite the travails. Recognizing the depths of intense fighting on many fronts, steeped in too many funerals, and too much mourning, we looked ahead to the national days of celebration and remembrance and wondered how we would be able face them again. We knew the days that are already painful, like Yom HaShoah and Yom HaZikaron especially, would be excruciating, as our most recent losses cast their shadows over everything. We contemplated the days that are meant to be joyful – Yom HaAtzmaut, Lag BaOmer, and Yom Yerushalayim – and bumped up against the tension between the days' celebratory nature and gratitude, on the one hand, and this season of suffering, on the other.

Our experience with *Az Nashir* has taught us that prayer allows us, even expects, us to imagine a different and better future, even when we feel unsure in the face of the journey to get there. We experienced how prayer opens new horizons in our souls. And we wanted to use the hopeful prism of prayer to ease our way through the emotional days of remembrance and celebrations ahead. We knew that others would have the words to unlock our hearts again, providing the language and sentiment to reframe our approach to these days. We looked to them to help us turn this season into a time for holding pain – and choosing hope.

And so we embarked on another whirlwind of workshopping and writing, getting ready for the new season.

One of the shining features of *Az Nashir: We Will Sing Again*, and one of which we are most proud, was its bilinguality – every *tefillah* was presented in both Hebrew and English, regardless of the language of composition. Identifying as we do as People of the Book, we cannot ignore the significance of our holy tongue, and as both Jews and Israelis, the lingua franca of our homeland is important to us. That said, we present *Az Nashir: Between Silence and Song* in English (with occasional lines in Hebrew).

We welcome you, holding this *siddur*-companion in your hands, not just as a reader, but as a reciter. Say these prayers with us. Know that you are not alone in holding the tension of grief and joy, mourning and celebration, fear and hope. By saying these prayers, you join a worldwide community of women who seek to connect with their deeper selves, with each other, with God, with our past, or with our future.

Reading the prayers in this volume may feel like sitting with another woman – a mentor, sister, or friend – who understands where you have been, what you feel, what you hope for, because she has felt it too. The writers represent a broad spectrum of voices that touch upon different life experiences, needs, and senses of what prayer can be. There are many ways to connect to the Divine.

While each of the prayers before you is personal and intimate, woven out of the innermost chambers of our hearts and the depths of our souls, publishing them allows us all to tune into a shared experience. It turns our personal yearnings, pleas, hopes, and dreams into a shared song.

Held by this communal song, we are comforted by each other and the presence of God.

May God hear and answer our pleas, while bringing the final redemption, speedily in our days.

Shira, Rachel, & Anne
Jerusalem, Spring 2025

Introduction

History of Women's Prayer Writing

This book follows an ancient tradition of religious Jewish women writing their own prayers.

The Jewish women of ancient Babylonia recited personal prayers spontaneously, from the heart, when they lit candles. Their practice traveled down the generations even to this day, among some Iraqi Jewish women.

The Jewish women in Spain after 1492, who were living as crypto-Jews, kept prayer alive for the community. When many prayers were lost because the Jewish community was exiled, the women attempted to collect as many prayers as they could recall. Wishing to pray as Jews, but having no access to the myriad Jewish books that had been destroyed, they often put together personal prayers orally based on what they could remember, adding words borne from their personal experiences.

In Ashkenazic tradition through the ages, Jewish women had a high level of literacy, especially and most comfortably in Yiddish. The Yiddish *mama-loshen* – mother tongue – was, therefore, the natural choice when the women wrote their own prayers, though most of our liturgy is in Hebrew and Aramaic. Starting in the Middle Ages, *techines* – contemporary Yiddish prayers – were written for the entire community by both men and women; many of those written by women were also written for women, detailing the most intimate parts of daily life. From lighting candles to entering the *mikveh* to crying out to God during labor, these prayers captured the essence of the emotional and spiritual depths of the female Jewish experience. Officially published in Prague from around the year 1600, *techinot* are still in use in Jewish homes all around the world, and the writing and reciting of them, for many, serve as a daily practice in their personal devotions to God.

In all these different locales and chapters of history, Jewish women found God in the details of their daily lives: the smell of the burnt challah offering before Shabbat, the warm waters of the *mikveh*, and their children's voices. As we can only aspire to step into their shoes, we seek the Divine in the old familiar places, as well as in our grandmother's recipes, in the natural world around us, in the healing we bring to the world through our work, the families we build, our relationships, our self-actualization even in moments of crisis, and what we create alongside God in partnership. The prayers in this book touch upon these contemporary experiences of daily life and more.

Jews and Personal Prayer

Our sages modeled our daily prayers on the prayer of one remarkable Jewish woman: Chana, mother of the prophet Shmuel. Determined to have a child, and refusing to heed her husband's advice to focus on "the silver linings," Chana offered God more than a burnt-offering; she entrusted her open heart and vulnerable words to Him. Chazal, the rabbis of the Talmud, were inspired by her manner of prayer when they structured our canonized prayers, but it was Chana's faith and vulnerability that continue to inspire generations of Jewish women. When we pray, we share Chana's conviction that God cares about innermost yearnings.

Chana's history-altering prayer brought about the birth of the prophet Shmuel, who led the people from the era of the Judges to the establishment of the Jewish kingdom. It is fitting that the biblical book that opens with Chana ends with King David, whose prayers convey the same pure faith in God's ability to intervene on his behalf. He channels the same honesty regarding his most authentic yearnings and needs into his personal conversations with God.

King David's words came alive for us since October 7th. As he describes in *Tehillim*/Psalms, there were times when we felt helpless, pathless, and stuck in despair. As we hid from armed and murderous invaders, buried loved ones, or huddled in shelters during the "*leilot shimurim*" (nights of

God's watchfulness) of rocket attacks, prayer became more than a personal practice. It became a way to grasp for hope.

Prayer implies faith in the possibility of something better. It was this faith that animated Miriam the Prophetess (according to the Midrash) when she instructed the Israelite women to prepare musical instruments before leaving Egypt, confident that there would be miracles to celebrate along the way. Perhaps, by reminding the people of this faith, these instruments offered the people solace even before the miracle took place.

We hope that the prayers before you offer comfort, in the spirit of Chana, David, Miriam, and all the generations of Jews who allowed themselves to hope for a better world.

Redemption of the Past, Redemption in the Future

It is said that the final redemption will mirror the redemption of the Jewish people from Egypt. That redemption is easy to remember in elation, but it was surely tremendous upheaval for the people. By singing in gratitude, Miriam and the women helped the people move past their passive confusion and shock and recognize the momentousness of their experiences.

In their preparedness to usher in the redemption of their generation, Miriam and the women model for us, the women of our current moment, what it looks like to be ready for redemption.

The sages taught that the generation of the Exodus was redeemed in the merit of the *"nashim tzidkaniot"* – righteous women. Knowing that we, as women living through this difficult time, have the opportunity to bring the redemption closer, we pray that by following in Miriam's footsteps, we hasten the arrival of all the blessings of *geulah*.

Women's Experience of the War and a Post-October 7th World

We have all encountered our brave new post-October 7th world in different ways, aware that it will not revert to what it was before that day.

Some women went out to fight. Some went to volunteer – with food and army gear, for those in need: soldiers, the wounded, the grieving, the displaced. Some spent their hours in advocacy, shouting to the world on behalf of the hostages and their families, fighting to bring our sisters and brothers home. Some were mired in grief, having lost beloved family, friends, community members, colleagues, acquaintances, fellow Jews or Israelis. We are all learning in our various ways how to live in a world that is broken and how to keep it from breaking us.

Many of us have sat with our own personal struggles against the backdrop of the national tragedies. Some of us felt we had no right to feel what we felt, or even to be present for ourselves, when so many around us were suffering. Some of us have been plagued by numbness or sadness. Many of us have been doing our best just to keep our heads above water. And then some of us have found deeper, more profound strength. Some have found new scope for leadership. Many of us have found ourselves with greater capacity for empathy. Our shoulders may be heavy with burdens, but we have found we can hold our heads high.

And most of us push ourselves, sometimes, just to keep going. Get our work done. Be there for our people. Living in an irregular time.

We have been all these women. As circumstances changed and shifted again, so did we, and so did our prayers. We hope that this new book of prayers will ease the many versions of yourself into the season of mourning and celebration, as we turn to the Divine, and help you navigate the tension inherent in these days that has increased in our post-October 7th world.

The thoughts of the heart are man's,
but from the Lord comes the utterance of the tongue. (Proverbs 16:1)

God,

Be with us in this moment of challenge,
For all the days that come before us,

That sometimes demand what feels
Hard to give.

Watch over all the souls You have taken,
The generations that will never come to be,
And the orphans and the widows
who demand the justice of Your love.

Soothe our grief,
And comfort the mourners among us,
For we all grieve
In the days of war.

Imbue our souls with
Your spirit,
So we may be lifted to the heights
Of Your days of celebrations.

Help us understand Your Divine plan,
Give us clarity around what still eludes us.
Bolster us with good news,
Set us all free from this suffering.

Shine Your light through Jerusalem,
Washing over the world with truth,
Let us hear the call of Your shofar
Heralding a new era of everlasting peace.

Amen.

Acknowledgments

Publishing *Az Nashir: We Will Sing Again* taught us in profound ways how books are group projects, and all the more so when the goal is to give voice to different people on different topics, even when the umbrella of prayer links them all. *Az Nashir: Between Silence and Song* is also the product of a loving collaborative, women who wrote from their hearts, and on strict deadline, to meet the need of the moment. We asked them to write in response and in preparation for one of the six significant times that these prayers honor, and, each according to her interest and experience, responded with poetry and pathos. They poured out their *tefillot* from the depths of their souls, and we are humbled to present them before you.

Our artists are amazing, offering generously the way they see the world, how they express the truth they perceive in their creative mediums. We are humbled to host your work among these pages.

A massive thank you to Yitzchak Woolf, who brought this book to life through his incredible cover design, typeset, and layout. It would not have been possible without your vision and creative energy.

We are especially grateful to our wonderful families, who encouraged us to take on this project – another one! – supported us through sleepless nights and last-minute stress, reminded us of our vision when we lost ourselves in the details, helped us keep our sanity through the rough patches, and celebrated our moments of success with cheerleading, generosity, and love.

And finally, as we come to the finishing touches, we are poignantly aware of the fact that we owe every moment of the relative calm that we were able to optimize for our efforts here to our soldiers, who, even now, are defending Israel and fighting to return safety to the land, to the families who support them from the homefront, as well as to all the others who have been attending to urgent matters and sacrificing so much for the immediate needs of our nation. And of course to *Hashem*, who aids them – and us – in this difficult time.

It is to all the men and women who protect Israel and help its denizens, both at the front and at home, that we offer this book, as we did the original *Az Nashir*, with gratitude and love.

Yom HaShoah

HOLOCAUST
REMEMBRANCE DAY

A Prayer for Yom HaShoah
The Editors

God,

It is hard to find the words to capture the horror.
We have heard the testimonies,
We have read the memoirs,
We have seen the lists and photographs and scars,
and yet, we still cannot comprehend the devastation.

In a history ridden with persecutions, pogroms, and massacres,
Still we cannot grasp the magnitude,
The breadth,
The genocide of Your people.

Gather to You,
The souls of the millions murdered
Men and women,
Children and babies,
Those whose names are known
And those whose names are lost to us.

Help us to remember eternally
The generation whose hatred for Your nation,
Spread like a fatal disease,
Enabled people of many countries,
All too eager to participate in murdering us.

Help us, the descendants of the survivors of this horror,
To hold the memories of our people sacred,
And help us continue to do good in their names,
Raising their souls through our deeds,
So they may continue to inspire Your work in this world.

May we be worthy custodians of their legacy.

Zakhor

Shira Lankin Sheps

God,

"*Zakhor*" is what my grandfather said to me on his deathbed,
His bright eyes focused on me, one last time,
"*Zakhor*" was written on a pin in my grandmother's jewelry box,
And now that she's gone, it rests in mine.

You have branded "*Zakhor*" on my back,
Stamped it on my brain,
Burned it into my DNA,
And I am unable to forget even if I wanted to.

You breathe "*Zakhor*" in and out of my lungs,
And it replays scenes I couldn't possibly remember,
Feels feelings of fear from someone else's lifetime.
You weave it into my nervous system, during mine.

You whisper "*Zakhor*" in my nightmares,
And I dream of dogs with fangs, hunting,
Broken glass, cutting,
The smell of smoke on the wind.

"*Zakhor*" is stories of people I should have met,
Of empty seats at the table,
Of being named for someone who was murdered,
Of being born to replace what was destroyed.

"*Zakhor*" highlights news headlines,
And brings out urgency
That belongs to generations ago,
But You are playing it out in my time.

"*Zakhor*" is swastikas on store windows,
Ripped-down posters of Your hostages,

Hatred from the left and the right,
Pogroms around the world this year.
You have sewn *"Zakhor"* in yellow on my chest,
It hangs with the Star of David on my neck,
Is worn with the map of Israel on my throat,
Is wrapped into the folds of the scarf on my head.

"Zakhor" is seeing the crisis when it comes,
And knowing the history of Your people cycles again and again.
It's recognizing that the only thing different today is Your land,
Realizing that for the first time in millennia, we can go home.

"Zakhor" is knowing that You remember too.
That You cry with us, too.
That You mourn for them, too.
That You love us, too.

Yizkor Am Yisrael

Michal Porat Zibman

Yizkor Am Yisrael,
Remember, nation of Israel.
Let us recall that before they were the six million, they were
individuals.
Before they were victims, they were people.
Yizkor Am Yisrael,
That before they were survivors, they were humans with passions and
dreams and hopes and beliefs and loves.
El Maleh Rachamim,
God filled with compassion,
Help us be an *Am Maleh Rachamim*
A nation filled with compassion.
And You are the God who is *Pokeach Ivrim*, the eye-opener.
So when I reflect on Auschwitz and Majdanek,
Let my eyes see not only the crematoria,
that burned their bodies.
Let us see the fire of passion that our ancestors had for their families,
their communities,
and their nation.
Pokeach Ivrim, Eye-opener,
Let me see,
envision,
And imagine
the individuals, the shuls, the schools, the teachers, the students, the
youth movement leaders, the rabbis, the women, the mothers, the
fathers, the grandparents…
the *Shabbas* tables, the yom tov *tefillot*, the excited students of Sarah
Schenirer, the chasidim going to their rebbes, the idealists of the
Bund, and the Zionists who loved *Eretz Yisrael*…

Yizkor Am Yisrael.
Let *Am Yisrael* remember.

Let *Am Yisrael* be remembered.

Let memory not remain in the past, but become meaning, mission,
    and purpose.
The mass graves of Warsaw, Zbilitovska Gura, Lupochowa… Let
    memory not remain only in a cemetery.

When we come upon the screaming silence of Treblinka, Belzec, and
    Sobibor,
Let us hear the *Shabbas zemirot*, the noisy classrooms, the shmoozing
outside the Nozyk Shul in Warsaw, the shul in Lancut, the Rema shul,
    and the temple in Cracow.
Let's raise our eyes to the train tracks that led the Jews to their final
    destination,
Let's stretch them to see where the tracks started from the
    communities, the synagogues, the homes, the *Shabbas* tables.

Let their legacy be not that they died,
But that they lived.
Not only how they died,
But how they lived.

God on High and God of Here
God of Why and God of Where

God of Then and God of Now
God of Again and God of How

El Maleh Rachamim
Why weren't these the *Achronim*, the last to die this way?
Our world needs some more of that *rachamim*, Your goodness
El Maleh Rachamim,
An *Am Maleh Rachamim* asks –
Bestow upon us the privilege of living in an
Olam Maleh Rachamim, a world of compassion and goodness.

May their memory be that before they were victims, they were human
    beings.

Zikhronam LiVerakhah
May their memories always be for a blessing.
May their memory enable blessing.

And in humility and awe, with heads held high,
Let us say, or shout, or cry, Amen.

Our Mother's Torah

Shoshana Judelman

Hashem,
My mother always worried about the ridges in her fingernails.
She was afraid of what it meant about her health, or what was coming.
One day, I saw the same manifestation on my own nails.
Mystery solved; it was genetic.
I had inherited my ridges, as she had likely inherited hers,
But this was not something she realized
Because she couldn't remember her mother's hands.
Her mother passed away nearly 70 years ago;
in the aftermath of the trauma,
There were other things to worry about besides fingernails.

In the blank spaces of the years that came before me,
Often it feels like my mother came out of nowhere.
And I, too, feel as if I was born of this void,
A teacher of Jewish history,
Always searching for my link in the chain,
That hangs suspended from vanished memories.

I am missing the transmission of more than trauma.
I am searching for a relationship with You,
Immersed in what I should have known,
Or had, or inherited,
What was snatched by years ravaged
By unimaginable loss, pain, and
The eradication of communities and families,
Who vanished from history
And left a gaping hole in their absence.

I received memories of horrors I never knew,
And an incomplete roadmap for how to find You.
I know how to keep Your Torah and follow Your *mitzvot*,

Because the knowledge housed in Your books survived.
And I can access that through my mind.
But the feeling of being hugged by my grandmother,
Was stolen from me.

And with those hugs should have come,
An intimate experience of You.
I should have tasted You in her cooking,
Internalized the *tefillah* of her daily chores.
She would have worn You sewn into her pockets,
She would have carried You in her hands.
But I hit a gap of transmission,
And cannot retrieve what was erased.

My yearning is focused:
A somatic need in a cerebral world,
To feel Your Presence through her,
To feel the warmth of Your loving embrace,
And pass it to my children through my bones,
Through my cooking,
Through my hands.

And I feel rendered mute,
Groping in the darkness,
desperately seeking relationship
and the fire of *tefillah*,
but finding only black and white words on a page.

I am stuck in my head,
when I know the pathway is through my heart.

And then I look again at my fingers,
If my DNA gave me ridges in my nails,
did it also give me more?
Do her prayers still call out to You from my veins?
Is it there, just beneath the surface,
waiting to be realized,
waiting to pour out of me?

Please, *Hashem*,
on this day and every day,
help us, we who have been orphaned by history and horror,
re-engage the Torah of our mothers,
and finally feel You.

Covenant
Anne Gordon

El Maleh Rachamim.

Dear God, who created the world
and blessed the Jewish people
with both exaltation and profound suffering,
please accept our faith in You,
even when we question Your ways,
even when we struggle with the idea that everything is for the best.

Cherish the souls and memories of
all the Jewish men, women, and children,
religious and secular, pious and irreverent,
and the non-Jews who suffered with us,
who were murdered on European soil and in its fires,
and wherever, however, they spread beyond,
at the hands of those who warped the *tzelem Elokim* that You placed in
      them,
replacing their humanity and compassion
with indifference, hatred, and desecration.

May we never forget the loss
of the innumerable worlds that were slaughtered in our recent past,
as we march forth with an appreciation for the essence of life,
with Jewish pride,
and with a sense of responsibility to live more fully,
a mandate to protect that gift,
and stand forthright in our resilience.

May we always identify Your covenant with us as a blessing,
for the thread of the nation that is eternally saved,
and upholds the memory of those who perished.

I Live This Life for You

Briana Grogin

Uziel Spiegel, an infant, wrapped in your mother's protective arms. In line to meet the devil himself, Dr. Mengele. Your grandmother, Rachel Rosenwasser, in an unimaginable split-second decision, took you at the last moment, so that your mother would be sent to the right, to life. You and your grandmother took your last breaths in the gas chambers of Auschwitz. I see your candle at Yad Vashem, an eternal flame mirrored back at me 1.5 million times for the other 1.5 million Jewish children who perished in the Holocaust.

Uziel and Rachel, I live this life for you.

Hennek, my uncle, and just a teenager/slave laborer at Auschwitz. You survived it all. You survived it all! The Nazis can hear the Americans approaching. Those monsters took you in the last days of the war and shot you in cold blood.

Hennek, I live this life for you.

Frida and Emil Koth and your 5-year-old son, Uziel, all terrorized and terrified on the train to Auschwitz. Frida, your brother somehow opened the cargo train door! People are jumping out to save themselves. You and your husband plead with the others to throw out your 5-year-old son and then you will follow, but no one is willing to take the chance with another person's life. All three of you remain frozen on the train until it reaches its deadly destination.

Frida, Emil, and Uziel, I live this life for you.

I am named for a woman I never met. Baila Majerovicz, my great-grandmother, stolen from her life. Baila, you were the mother of three beautiful children. You were in the hospital recovering from surgery. The Nazis took their easiest, most defenseless victims first. The place of healing became a death trap.

Baila, I live this life for you.

My grandparents, Hela and Henry Roven, of blessed memory, survived these horrors. I grew up on stories half-told. The blank stares that would sometimes take over, those eyes had seen too much. They spoke of courage and survival, and left out the traumatic wounds, too dark to put into words.

I learned young that Hitler's persecution of "Jew" was broader than we could have imagined. Even those who renounced their Jewish identity were still marked. If they were murdered for simply being Jews, then I dedicate my life to simply being a Jew.

I searched. I dove into the question: What does it mean to be a Jew? What is the *neshamah* of a Jew? My search led me on an insatiable journey. The more I learned, the more I wanted to learn.

I learned that, throughout history and until the present day, the Jewish people are a people of moral clarity who rise from the ashes stronger than before, and bring light to the world.

Now I walk the streets of my own land, my homeland. I raise my children in a country where being Jewish is celebrated, where words of Torah are heard on every street corner. I breathe the fresh, holy air of Jerusalem. And on Yom HaShoah, when we stand in silence, we mourn and we remember. Fully, proudly, unshakably Jewish, living in our ancestral land of Israel.

We are living this life for you.

Children of Memory: Inspired by Roman Vishniac | *Avigail Wieder*

A Prayer from the Depths:
A Theology of Suffering for Yom HaShoah

Etta Bendavid

Hashem,

On this Yom HaShoah, I recall the vastness of evil perpetrated against our already numbered nation. An evil that annihilated countless communities of Jews during the Shoah. I reflect on the names of towns and cities that have been captured on tombstones in Treblinka – most of them completely eradicated. I quiver at the images of mass graves, cemented on my mind and in my heart. I tremble at the piles of ash, once human beings, all of them, our ancestors. Each person was a whole world. My heart aches considering the abundance of light, love, righteousness, and wisdom that was brutally stolen and obliterated.

Today, God, of all days, with agonizing love, pain, and anger, we seek You out. As we remember the valleys of the shadow of death that our people endured, we urge You to do so, too. As the Eternal Witness, remember our endless struggle. Recall and embrace every single Jewish soul killed for being a Jew, and the righteous gentiles who tried to save us, too.

Today, of all days, God, may You move from Your transcendent throne and draw near to us with Your immanence and Your shelter. Take an accounting of us, pleading on behalf of Your voiceless children. For Your sake, God, we seek Your reassurance, and Your resilience to strengthen us.

In the shadows of the October 7th massacre, we glimpse the horrors of the Shoah and wonder how we continue to endure this torture, dear God. This covenant between us, *Hashem,* is suffused with suffering. Together, let us recall Your servant, our grandfather, *Avraham Avinu,* who acquired a covenant inscribed with oppression: When Avraham turned to You before Yitzhak was even conceived and asked, "How am I going to KNOW, God, that You will keep Your promise – that You will bless us with countless descendants, and give us *this* Promised Land – when I don't even have one son!?" You told him that his descendants will first suffer in a land that is not theirs. It will be a long road ahead, You said. Our covenant was guaranteed to carry suffering and blessing together. That is when our struggle began.

Shema Yisrael, Hashem! Listen to Your people, who will always and forever wrestle with You, *Hashem*, until the coming of *Mashiach*. Listen to Your children, the dead and the living, as we declare Your Oneness.

Every night at bedtime, I sing this *tefillah* to my children, in the hopes that Your words protect them; remind them that You are close to them, God. I pray You'll watch over my children, and I surrender them to You in the most vulnerable hours.

This same *Shema Yisrael* was wailed and whispered to You, God, throughout the Shoah, when six million Jews, and among them, one-and-a-half-million children, were sent to their deaths.

Did You hear them, *Hashem*, Judge, Father, King, *Shekhinah, Shadai, Elokim?*
Did Your Presence shelter them in their final moments?
Did You reassure those dying that they were not alone?
Did You cover the children with Your warmth and whisper to them to soothe them when they were covered in dirt, blood, bullets and ash?
I remind You, God, but I don't need to. You don't forget. You remember everything.

We seek You out now, like Rivka our matriarch, who, in her agony, was the first to ask "Why?" and demanded an answer from You directly.

We seek You out now because *Ya'akov Avinu* taught us to lean into the pain. He taught us that our name "Yisrael" means to grab hold of our wounds and demand a blessing. Yisrael means so much more than to grapple with God and man. The only way we will prevail is by following in Yaakov's actions. To be Yisrael means to struggle and to prevail by bravely grabbing hold of the pain for dear life, tightening our grip, and demanding *berakhot*, blessings.

Dear God, strengthen us to pursue blessings, and fill us with the power of perspective to fight for our future, to visualize the redemption to come, in the form of joy, victory, *nachat*, and peace. Help us inhabit the namesakes of our people – *Ivri* (courage to be different), *Yehudi* (courage to thank), *Yisrael* (courage to struggle and demand blessings) – to acknowledge our oscillating narrative of persecution and perseverance. Grant us the wisdom to simultaneously teach our children of our past full of darkness and light, while we fight for our destiny, with joy and passion and strength.

Please God, for Your sake, save our people.

As for me, I will forever continue to cry to You and sing to You.
To demand Your blessings, Your gaze, and Your answers.
For good.
For Your people.
For Your sake.

Amen.

The Abyss of Memory

Yael Shahar

My God,
When memory overwhelms
And defeat is all we face…

We stand on the edge of the abyss,
across whose unknowable face we paint meaning
so as not to see into it.
It is always there.
It will always be there.

The darkness covers us
Consigns us to oblivion
Steals our unshed tears
The memory of our father's voice
The feel of our mother's hand on our head
The abyss takes its due.

But, God of memory,
Let us never devalue what we have lost.
Help us to remember the eternity hidden in our transience
The strength in our brokenness.
When memory threatens to overwhelm us
Let us remember that what is fragile is no less worthy for all that.

And when memory claims us
Allow us to mourn without bitterness.
Let us know the relief of tears shed without shame.
Allow us to grieve without losing our way in grief.
To stand against hatred without becoming what we fight.

When our humanity is trodden in the dirt,
Let us dust it off, mend the tatters,
And cherish it in its brokenness.

Having stood at the abyss
Let us not forget that the darkness is not all there is.
Having seen what none should have to witness
May we not forget that there is joy in the here and now.

The abyss remains…
But we are here too, and we are no less real than the abyss.
We are no less meaningful for being ephemeral creatures
caught up in something too big for us.

Help us, God of memory, to remember
The wholeness of a broken heart.
And may we hold fast to this knowledge
That those things that are most fragile are also the most precious.

Yom HaZikaron

A Prayer for Yom HaZikaron
The Editors

El Maleh Rachamim,

Please cherish the souls
and memories of all the men, women, and children,
Jews and non-Jews,
religious and secular,
Israelis and tourists,
who were murdered in acts of terror
and those who fell in battle
since the Jewish people's historic return to this land that You
dedicated to us,
thousands of years ago,
where we established the modern State of Israel.
The cost has been dear.

Please remember and redeem
all those we lost on October 7th,
and in the war since –
women and men,
children and the elderly,
civilians and soldiers.

From those who were murdered
in the coldest of cold blood on that black, black day,
to those who were taken captive and slain in captivity
in the many months since.

From those who left their families
and their festive Shabbat and Simchat Torah
to rush to the aid of those under brutal attack,
and were killed even as they saved others,

To the reservists who left their families to return to the battlefields,

and paid for their commitment to the people of Israel with their lives,
to the regular soldiers, young men and women at the cusp of
     adulthood,
who gave up their futures
for the sake of the nation's everlasting presence in this land.

Oh God,
we pray that we mourn these precious souls as they deserve,
and that their memories live on through us.

May we do good in the world, in their merit.

Yom HaZikaron: Remembering My Brother, Michael | *Avital Sharansky*

A Psalm of Har Herzl

Jessica Levine Kupferberg

On a rainy winter's day on this mountain of memory,
as fog spokes span over the golden city below and beyond –
I turn towards the *Har HaZeitim* and sing to You
a song of *Har Herzl*:

Hymn of roots, seeds, earth;
Past, present, future;
Elegy, psalm, celebration –
the march of a nation in weathered, heavy boots
treading paths of muck once more.

Even now and especially here,
chiffon almond blossoms stand sentinel around
monuments of Shoah, sacrifice, and dream –
a trio I understand so much better since that October rain
soaked us to the bone.

Since then, I have stood on Kibbutz Be'eri's blackened clay;
fallen down holes of our stolen who cannot return;
at long last stood on Auschwitz's ground
and recited words I sewed into a poem where my grandmother
once sewed garments of survival;
– and here, on this mountain,
I walked passed an endless flame
to a place of white bricks, solemnly staggered,
rows freshly etched with so many young, familiar names –
October's arm already stretching too far.

I have also seen the deepest dangers thwarted by Your hand;
laughed as a granddaughter born in a ceasefire learned to crawl;
danced at weddings of warriors; and
felt the clang of hammers in my veins, as I glimpsed soldiers helping
rebuild Kfar Aza, home by home and hope by hope.

And oh, to witness the greatest light emerging
from the darkest of tunnels, so bright it blinds us at first:
    Sagui learning his child bears the name "Mazal!" –
    a blast from Daniella's secret song of strength –
    the pluck of the strings of Agam's unshakable faith and Liri's lyre
    of courage –
    the leathered straps of gratitude wound 'round the arms of Ohad
    and Omer –
    a sip of wine from Keith's kiddush, so new and bittersweet:
    Shehechiyanu.

In this unmooring mix of thorn and honey, I humbly ask:
    When will we at long last be able to say, like Emily:
    "We are back to our beloved lives" –
    When will we truly feel again that we are free people in our land?

In this time, when the wings that carry us
can seem more butterfly than eagle
– gossamer, fragile, beautiful –
Oh, *Hashem!* Please gather our broken pieces and hug us to Your chest,
clear the fog and lift us up in flutters to see the distant views
– from this mountaintop, to Your mountaintop –
We are trying!
We are trying!

When the three days of Shoah, Sacrifice, and Dream
arrive standing side by side and then back to back
with the advent of Spring's pink buds of redemption,
through our red-headed tears and with faith under our fingernails
please help us learn from this mountain
how to hold it all at once,
how a heart that has only three fingers now
can still grasp joy and miracles fully and
only drop them when we wish –
only when we can plant them like song seeds over bone into ready earth.

We will it and yet still we dream.

First Bloom | *Leah Luria*

A Prayer for Mother's Eyes
Juliana Brown

("Ani einayim" *is the phrase used by military observers,* tatzpitaniyot, *as they hand over the watch, with the new soldier on duty taking over the screen from the previous soldier on duty. Until the incoming soldier says these words out loud, the outgoing soldier, who has been watching the screen until this point, is forbidden from moving her eyes away or relaxing her vigilance.*)

On my bed by night,
In the black silence of every night,
I am eyes-on. *Ani einayim.*
Mother's eyes.
My soldier daughter's voice rang out of the north
In the dark
Her friends, her *mefakedet* (commander), taken in the fiery storm of
     October
And I, in my home.
Vayehi be-chatzi ha-laylah.
(And it was in the middle of the night)
I remain eyes-on – vigilant – from that day, that moment, frozen
in the echo of her words over the phone. Her tears.
Every night, I wake with her beloved voice in my head, "*Ima…*"
     (Mom…)
There is so little comfort.
Her story returns to me over and over.
So I wake to watch.

This is the crushing weight of vigilance of our mothers in Egypt.
Aneinu (answer us).
Of Miriam charged with watching her brother's basket and his life –
     our lives.
Don't look away. *Aneinu.*
Of mothers driving their soldier-children to the train on Sunday

morning and whispering, "Be safe" into their sweet heads. *Aneinu.*
Of *Rachel Imenu* protecting from the roadside,
of Esther – the eyes inside the palace –
And of Yael, watching the final slumber of the enemy.

We are tired.
God of Israel, of mothers and daughters,
Take this watch now: *Tihyeh einayim,* be eyes-on.
And I will gratefully and gently lay down our burden before You.

And on this day, as we recount the stories of those
Gone from us in service of Your land, of Your nation,
As we speak their names to ourselves quietly at night,
Who shall we trust if not You? Lord of broken mothers.
Our eyes are closed to life beyond living,
Will You watch us with mother's eyes?

A Prayer for the Ones We Lost and for Ourselves

Rachel Sharansky Danziger

Lord of Hosts
You, Who know the innermost workings of our spirits,
You know who lives in my heart:
The ones we lost.
The ones we buried.

You know who leans against my lungs when I hug my children
choking me with borrowed longing
for they – the fallen – will never hug their own.

You know whose eyes look at me through my own eyes in the mirror
eyes that live in reflections, pictures, and memories
and tell me – live! Live, live, please live, for we cannot.

You know. You have watched me – us – mourn together.
You have watched me – us – cry over graves.
You have watched us holding hands and feeling the phantom of lost
hands between our fingers
as we dig into the land
and make wells of yearning
and cup their water in our palms
and drink.

We drink with their lips and bleed their tears and laugh at jokes they
would have said
had they but been here –
had they but been here
in the flesh.

Lord of Hosts and hearts and spirits,
You, Who know the hidden places of our hearts
You, Who know that we can never come to You alone

For they are with us
Always –

Please.
Dig into the earth of Your bountiful compassion.
Make a well into Your gifts of healing.
Cup the water of Your love
and let us drink.

Let us drink,
For every surface is a wound of remembrance.
Every bus stop an agglomeration of memories.
Every smiling face a reminder of another.
And we don't want to lose them
never lose them –

Help us carry them into our lives.
Help us live with them within us.
Help us do so without drowning in distress
and grief.

Lord of Hosts and memories,
Make their spirits within us a blessing.
Make our lives a continuation of their work.
Make the memories sing through us
and seep into the work we do in this universe,
make them nourish it
like the water feeds the growing tree.

Never Forget, Never Forgotten | *Inbal Singer*

Bless Us to See Each Other Again

Sarah Sassoon

God, I am seeking a bridge
from this world
to the next.

We have the materials
stone river water metal trees
but it is not with a hammer or nails
      it is not with bricks formed from the riverbanks
      it is more from longing
          from seeking
          love
      it is more from death
          and life
how we cross this bridge built of ash,
tears, seeds, stone.

God, You planted evil in man's hearts
and courage and love.

So many parts to hold in one heart
wild sage, seeping through the cracks.

Remember why we live
why they died.

We don't know how to hold this empty space
a burial ground
such an empty space of who we used to cradle in our arms,
safe.

I cannot protect my sons
but You can.

Are You with those who have died?

Are You here in war?

Did You exile us from the dream, the Garden of Eden
or did we exile ourselves?

It has always been about returning

every single day

is that what faith is?

To believe in the memorial candle I light
though empty twenty-four hours later
with a touch of wax memory at the bottom.
It's hard to remove
hard to un-remember
light.

Are we meant to return to the earth
fill up the memorial glass cup with all we are
dust of this earth,
and plant a seed
because we are of this earth
which birthed the tree of knowledge
good and bad.

We forgot to eat from the *Etz HaChayim*, the Tree of Life
We forgot how to live
so we plant seeds in an empty glass cup

and we shudder and shake with each siren.

Each siren, a reminder like a ram's horn
the ragged broken breath *teruah*-shout calling
from within

good and bad

bless us

to see each other again

bless us

to hold onto all we don't know
and don't understand

the empty spaces
of sons and daughters
and fathers and mothers

who we want to hold again
but can only plant a seed for
the ground they are buried in.

A young widow sits on her husband's
military grave and whispers to him
as she rubs her pregnant belly.

God, they died for us to live.

Teach us how to live.

Choose life, You say
and the angels sing, *holy holy holy.*
It's hard to hear the angels
in the graveyard.

Please let us learn Your song
of angels praising seventy faces
        seventy languages
the sacred language of seeds in a mother's womb.

I do not know how to comfort the mothers
I hug his mother
she will always be the fallen soldier's mother.
The Blood of the Maccabee flowers pinned on blouses,
blossom with each generation.

How is it sadness births beauty
      pain births gratitude.

How is it the foundation stone of Your home
is planted with tears
of joy and pain.

Oh God, hear our memorial sirens
our *teruah* calls for
all we have lost
to protect
all we still have.

Please help us learn to bless every step on this earth
sown with tears and blood and bones.
Let there always be children's laughter
and ancient songs sung on the streets of Jerusalem.

Please guide us, hold us, bless us
as we cross this narrow, fragile bridge
from today until tomorrow
all we mourn all we celebrate
between worlds
life and death and living
let us remember it helps to hold hands

remember this
remember them.

In Lament and Fear: A Prayer for Protection

Anne Gordon

May I always remember, O Lord,
To turn to You in thanksgiving,
When Israel is quiet.
When the air does not ring with sirens, when no cars jump the curbs,
when I don't scan crowded places for a quick exit,
and the "suspicious objects" are no more than kids' forgotten
      backpacks.

I would plead with You too, God of my ancestors,
Who has protected so many,
To keep those who spread terror away from Your nation.
The Jewish people have suffered enough.
When this evil flourishes on our outskirts,
or is released from our gates,
It cruelly resurrects the terror that…
killed and maimed and terrified (as it was designed to do).
Please, God, prevent the many layers of cruelty
Spawned by such willful inhumanity.

I don't really remember Entebbe (I was only six),
But I remember my mother crying (was it the first time I saw her cry?).
A friend's parents were on the plane.
And she took the call in ignorance,
Becoming wise only to the fact that they
(her friend, herself, the entire world)
Were waiting, waiting, waiting…
Until the Israeli commandos rescued them,
those first hostages of my memory.
The ones I don't really remember,
Who introduced the waiting of terror to me.

I don't remember Munich at all (I wasn't even three).

But the Olympics were colorful, musical, sporting.
The annual brief showing of the shadowy video of masked gunmen
who slaughtered
Israeli athletes
Shattered the fanfare and good cheer.
Even as an echo of past terror.
Those days should have been freed of politics.
Freed of violence.
Freed of hatred.
Nothing is sacred.

Not even the sacred.
On Sukkot (it was 1990), the rocks came over the Wall with abandon.
Jerusalem stone is heavy.
It takes effort to hoist and hurl and harm
Those praying below.
The blessings of the priests – may they always come to pass –
Were interrupted,
The plaza cleared.
To hit us in prayer –
Not the first, nor last terror of its kind –
Will You prevent the terror when we no longer can pray
        for Your salvation?

I review a "List of Palestinian suicide attacks."
It says the list is not comprehensive.
An incomplete list of 161 suicide bombings.
Too many murdered (any is too many)
whom we mourn today.
They don't all kill. But they're supposed to.

They weren't all buses.
But so many were buses:
Afula, Hadera, Dizengoff, Jerusalem,
Kfar Darom (you know, before the Disengagement),
Ramat Gan (that's near Tel Aviv), Ramat Eshkol (that's Jerusalem)

Jerusalem. Ashkelon. Jerusalem again. That long, long route of the
    Number 18 – and tempting, hitting the same line again.
Dizengoff again.
Tel Aviv. Gush Katif. Ben Yehudah, Machane Yehudah
    (Jerusalem, my right hand won't lose its cunning).
The list, we know, is incomplete.

Shall I run for the bus?
It might be the most important decision of my life.
Shall I spring for a taxi?
Does that let the terrorists win?
Or is it prudent, wise, safe-guarding
Ourselves and well-being.

Keep your wits about you, spot the suspicious objects, and
foil the slaughter by five buses
(Were they supposed to detonate during rush hour? Were they
    supposed to kill hundreds?)
Do we tell our children to stop taking the bus?
Do we interfere with their freedom? Reduce their independence?
Is this the most important decision of our lives (God forbid)?
Do we chauffeur them? Taxi them?
Is that letting the terrorists win?
(We can't function if we don't protect our children)
Would it be so hard to guarantee their safety? Oh, please!

Thank You, God, for the attacks that fail.
For the attacks that do less harm than the enemy's goals.
That do no physical harm.
(We'll keep working on our resilience)

We know – we trust, we believe, we know – You will uphold Your
    promise,
And the remnant will always survive.
But what of the losses? The families torn asunder,
by the cruelty that attacks with intent to destroy
(and succeeds; even one is too many)

We all want to survive.
Please stop the terrorists before they harm.
We want to shed this suffocating coat of fear, of mourning.
Abate our sorrow, redeem our trust.
Please, God, overturn the terrorists and their goals –
Like Sodom and Gemorra.
Will that require fire and brimstone?
Like Nineveh.
Might they return to You instead?
(if they do, we'll relax our vengeance)
But not our anguish.
Nor our mourning.

On this day, when we remember our fallen,
        the soldiers on the battlefields, yes,
And our civilians who battled for peace,
Slain with the coldest intent of cold blood,
As they'd continued along, in good faith,
Refusing to let the terrorists win.
Their deaths have been numerous
(We remember. One is too many)
May there be no more.

O dear God who is full of mercy,
You who allow us to make sense of Your world,
Grant us generations of peace in Your land.

A Prayer for the Victims of October 7th
Shira Lankin Sheps

God,
We cannot understand
The infamous 7th day that fractured our world,
The storm that broke through the supposed sea walls,
And flooded the land,
Drowning everything as we knew it.

Was the world not meant to rest on the seventh day?
A day for dancing and celebration of Your Torah?
Instead, a whole world,
Drowning by sirens, and we,
Late to respond to the call,
Fighting to get down there,
As we plunged into the depths of chaos.

On that day Your people were murdered,
Plundered, raped,
Picked off from the kibbutzim,
Mid-dance at the festival,
Babies in their cribs,
Animals shot,
Families sheltering each other
Houses, fields, and bodies burned,
Beyond recognition.

In our grief, we replay their final moments,
The stories we've learned,
The testimonies we've heard,
The video footage we cannot erase from our minds,
We could not have imagined the terror.

They laughed while they defiled us,
They exulted while they mutilated us,

They exclaimed while they murdered us,
Where is the answer from the heavens??

All Your people wanted to do
Was dance,
Was sleep,
Was build,
Was play,
Was plant,
Was love,
Was pray,
Was make peace.

May we remember them, that way, always.

May You remember them,
Gathered up in Your arms,

Create an Eden for their goodness,
Where they can rest under Your protection,
For all eternity.

בדמייך חיי: In Your Blood, Live | *Bracha Lankin*

A Prayer for the Hostages Murdered in Captivity

Shira Lankin Sheps

God, it is hard to know
What is a man-made mess,
Or what You have planned.
You know all,
The past, present, and future
And yet we know that living in this world
Requires effort and endeavor.
Our choices affect reality
But who would have chosen this?

Salachtanu, forgive us, that we did not bring them home alive,
Though we waited and prayed,
Negotiated and advocated,
Pricked and protested,
Searched and fought,
Lost many precious lives of our soldiers
To bring them home.

God, why?
Why did their stories have to end this way?
Why? When we waited so long to see them,
Counted the days 'til they should have been
Reunited with their loved ones,
In the embrace of their families.
Home in their country.

And now if we are lucky, we get caskets
Instead of embraces,
Precious bodies whose souls have left this plane of existence,
Who have surely reached the highest levels of heaven
Watching over us, their testimonies demanding

That You bring them all home, once and for all?

While we have been fighting this venomous snake
That weaves its poison through innocents,
Which spawns new evils the world won't watch,
We fight, and weep, we scream, and we keep pushing,
Whispering the names of the taken under our breaths,
Hanging their pictures on banners,
Touching their sketched faces on our bus stops,
And on every wall in Your holy cities, we write,
"We're sorry!!"
"Forgive us!!"
For we are lost in this hideous maze,
Of tunnels dug into darkness,
And we are desperately trying to climb out,
And bring everyone out with us.

We need Your help!
As we always have.
Help us bring the rest home.
Take them out with an outstretched arm,
Leave not one body, not one soul left with them,
Grant our dead the sanctity of burial in their homeland,
In Your land,
For they were stolen for Your sake.

When You receive them in Your holiest of courts,
Let their stories shake the heavens and earth,
Be zealous in their honor,
In Your name,
Act in their names,
Restore justice to this world that You created,
And return peace and prosperity to Your people,
To Your holy land.

May the souls of the hostages who were murdered in captivity,
Sit by Your throne,

Held close to You,
Saved from earthly sorrow,
And may their families be ensconced in Your embrace,
The embrace owed to them,
Comforted among the mourners of Zion.

Holy One Blessed be He,
The hostages who are still in the land of the living,
And those who have passed to the next world,
Leave not one left behind.
Bring them all home.

The Seeds of Hope

Sarah Ansbacher

In the flames of destruction, our prayers ascended.
We cried to You: Please do not forsake us.
Our land laid waste.
We feared it was the end.
But ashes nurtured the soil and planted seeds of hope.

A remnant watched its people –
Fleeing east
Taken west
Slaves in chains forced to serve the empire of destruction,
But carrying with them the seeds of hope.

Blood libels, Crusades, Inquisition,
Expulsions, Pogroms, Farhud,
Holocaust.
Our prayers ascended in the flames
We cried to You: Please do not forsake us.
We feared it was the end
But we clung to the seeds of hope.

And in our land bereft
A remnant waited through time…
Conqueror after conqueror,
Generation after generation,
Watering the earth with their tears.

In the east and in the west
There was not a day we did not pray to return home to our land.
We never forgot.
Then we arose and returned –
On rickety boats,
On eagle's wings,
Carrying the seeds of our hope.

Out of the ashes, watered by our tears,
Seeds became saplings,
Saplings became trees,
Trees became forests.
The land bloomed.

In fields of bright flowers
We raised our flag
We sang our song of hope
And we prayed for peace.

But peace is elusive.
They cut down our flowers, our saplings, our trees.
Again, and again, and again,
Over, and over, and over again.

Fields of flowers that swayed in the autumn breeze,
Saplings cut down in their prime,
Trees that gave shade.
Two flame trees just starting to bloom,
A mother's song stolen from her lips.

In the flames of destruction, our prayers ascend,
We cry to You: Please do not forsake us.
Our tears water the earth
They extinguish the flames.
From fields laid waste, new buds emerge.

Mercy

Sherri Mandell

God, are we supposed to have Your eyes?
The long view,
The extended silence,

The exalted majesty.

The zoom-out
So that everything becomes smaller
And more manageable –
Even death.

Which is just a stop on Your railroad?
I imagine You, God, holding a pocketwatch
Calling out names
Like destinations.

We are supposed to believe that You are the conductor,
The driver and the train –
all of it under Your power.
We're at the station waiting

Straining to hear the music of Your wheels.

Tekes Ma'avar

A CEREMONY MARKING THE TRANSITION FROM
YOM HAZIKARON TO YOM HAATZMAUT

A Prayer for the Tekes Ma'avar
The Editors

Dear God of balance and bridges,

Here we stand in the epicenter of transitions
Holding both grief and gratitude,

For we know that all we have
Is due to those who gave their lives.

God, hold our hands
As we cross between the past and the future.

Bring with us their memories, their everlasting legacies
As we recommit to this nation we are still building.

Help us weave together
Who we have been and who we need to be.

Help us carry
Both our pain and our joy.

Teach us to live
With all these truths embedded in our hearts.

Lift us up from mourning,
Bring our legs to life as You dance with us.

Wipe away the sadness from our eyes,
Let us see all the good You have given us.

Fill us with thanksgiving,
And may we find satisfaction in the blessings of our present.

May You continue to watch over the people of Israel:
May You come among us to comfort us.
May You shine a light to lead us.
May You bring forth the final redemption, speedily, in our days.

We Are One Nation

Talia Haber

This prayer is לעילוי נשמת my husband, Dr. Zechariah Haber z"l, and all the soldiers, police, and civilians killed by Hamas in this war.

Hashem.
We came together.

Please remember October 8, when we eagerly volunteered and jumped to help each other, almost half of all Israelis began volunteering those first few terrifying days and money poured in from abroad.

Please remember the Jewish men who left their honeymoons to save other Jews – some who never came back home to their wives.

Please remember the Israelis who opened their homes to house evacuees.

Please remember the Jewish, Muslim, and Christian soldiers and police who died defending Israel, and all the volunteers, cowboys, doctors, and soldiers who flew in to help Israelis.

Please remember when close to 300,000 people converged on Washington, DC, to march for Israel – and comparable events around the world.

Please remember when soldiers on leave met up at the *kipah* store because they lost their *kippot* in Gaza.

Please remember the "secular" Jewish soldiers who survived a round in Gaza and said, "There is no greater feeling than re-entering Israel."

Please remember the heartfelt prayers of soldiers serving Chanukah, Purim, Pesach, Shavuot, Yom Kippur, and again Chanukah and Purim in Gaza.

Please remember the comedians and influencers who advocated for Israel.

Please remember the overflowing piles of *mishloach manot* outside the doors of injured *chayalim* (soldiers) and bereaved families.

Please remember the surviving comrades who act like fathers for the surviving orphans, escorting them to school and giving them piggyback rides.

Please remember the thousands of individuals who came to pay respects to people they care for and know all about – whom they never met.

Please remember the hundreds of *chesed* initiatives each bereaved family and I received – from the gentle soldiers who first knocked on our cold door, to the 4-year-old whose mom told me his son lights a Shabbat candle for my husband's memory, to the high-schoolers who stop by, asking to hear stories about my husband, to the insurance agents who volunteer to review insurance policies, to *tzedakah*, to the daily lunches and dinners my neighbors prepare for my kids and me, to other bereaved families who offer support, and all the people who have helped in their unique ways.

Let us stay together and keep helping each other.

Hashem
We saw You:

When no other bordering army joined Hamas to invade Israel.

When Rachel Edri baked her irresistible cookies.

When a soldier threw his comrade a pair of *tzitzit* and an enemy thought it was a grenade and fled.

When Chabad houses set up a *tefillin* stand and a menorah illuminating Gaza.

When my husband's *tefillin* were with him in the tank, yet returned home kosher.

When we left our saferooms before Pesach and before Rosh

Hashanah, shaking because the defense industry managers who had only guaranteed "no more than 90% success" – then delivered 99.9% success.

When the IDF successfully rescued some hostages.

When couples who battled separately on different fronts, apart for months of fear, rejoined each other.

When soldiers who left the battlefield and, despite rush-hour traffic, made it on time to the delivery room.

When soldiers who were not expected to survive began walking again.

When Israel saw extraordinary military successes detonating beepers in Hezbollah, destroying entire squadrons in Syria, and running missions and assassinations deep in Iran.

We saw You on the homefront when we saw bus bombs explode and no one was hurt, rockets at kindergartens when no one was there, and when terror attacks targeting Jews all over the world were thwarted before calamities.

Hashem.
We are still looking for You:

In the massacres of October 7th and the parties, homes, roads, and fields from which people were incinerated or taken.

In the rat-infested tunnels, wondering where the hostages are.

In the hospitals, where amputees wait for ghost limbs to be reattached, and in the PTSD clinics, where soldiers and survivors hope for healing.

In the eyes of those who are home physically, but mentally are still in Gaza.

In the abandoned communities waiting for their residents to return, and in the displaced families waiting to go home.

At the negotiating table, where we are extorted to pay exorbitant, dangerous sums.

In the surge of military cemeteries and memorials this year.

In the classrooms and workplaces to which teachers and colleagues never returned.

In the shiva houses of young soldiers and newlyweds who never had kids and in those where a family's dad and husband will never come home.

We hope You see us and how much we are there for each other – and hopefully, we can continue doing for each other.

We see You and how much You do protect us. We beseech You for more. We want to see You in all the pain of the war. We want to stop cycling between fear, hopelessness, and grief.

May we be able to live here and everywhere, supporting each other, continuing to be an inspiration to the world, and continuing to build and raise our families in peace.

The Burnt Tree | *Leah Jacobson*

A Prayer for Music, Movement, and the Winds of Change

Rachel Weinstein

The chaotic sway of arms and legs
Rising and falling under darkened clouds
Perform this frenzied dance.
I hold tightly to the melody and the unsteady rhythm
That has not spared me from fractures and falls.

In my angst, I tiptoe between raindrops
Afraid to feel the rush of water on my skin
Because life is already so saturated,
Heavy and pounding against the hatches of my mind.

Blessed God, I am not built for this relentless dance between the
        drops,
Swaying to and fro between torture and release
Sashaying from despair to faith, frightfully leaping
Until I'm stripped to the bare, soaked bones of my soul

Oh Holy One Who is Blessed and blesses us,
I beseech You tonight, change the chords and the lyrics
For we have been forced to dance to the music of affliction for far too
        long.

Right now, as the music shifts and the notes
Carry me higher,
Higher,
Higher still

I can see You and feel You
As the song reminds me that You reign.

I pray for peace that extends beyond yellow ribbons and Never Again's
Where blue and white flags burst through like sunshine

And dance along the winds of change.

Tomorrow, I will be wrapped in my flag's embrace
Skipping wildly through the puddles and fields
Where I pray poppies bloom in peace.

One day, I will dance in a world where I can fully rejoice
In the promise and deliverance of Your light, and love, and song —
Again, and again, and again.

The Asking

Yael Unterman

I

Master of the Universe
we do not believe You are
some uninvolved clockmaker
a "create-and-run" God
who made humans and then
   threw them under the bus.
No. You infuse our every pore
give us life at every moment
and there are things You also ask of us.

You ask of us
to be strong Jews, love the Torah
never despair,
love and serve You, cherish the laws,
be moral, always care.

And Your most intimate demand:
to control our very desires
our innermost emotions
our most personal authenticity.

For me this is not easy
as I live my unique humanity,
You ask me to bind
   my heart on the altar
to let the sacred fire take up my "I"
in a cloud of sweet-smelling smoke to the sky.

Please bless me to find
   the strength not to falter
to remain me while serving You faithfully.

II

Creator of the Universe
from You
we've learned to ask of ourselves,
we Jews

We ask ourselves to surrender our feelings
we demand of ourselves to bravely pivot
to fiercely turn our faces away
(as the angel demanded of Lot and his wife)
from a raw day of graves and memories
of huddled struggling families
gathering strength from the telling of stories.

As a gentle veil is drawn by twilight's
pink hues over a time of grief
that blanketed our souls in dull grey

We ask of ourselves the impossible:
to, like Joseph, dash from pit to pinnacle
in a miniscule moment;
throw off our heavy shrouds
face forwards, rise like the sun,
vaporize the clouds.

Now! Come on! Hearts wide!
Turn to the light
raise your antennae
locate the gift, the gratitude
rejoice! you have so much!

See – our beautiful land is ours again
after 2,000 years!
Dance like a wildflower in the rain,
release the pain, dry your tears!
Make a barbecue, sing old songs,

go for hikes, chant Hallel!
Fling your arms around each other
in a joyful *Hora*!
Swing an inflatable hammer
and bop your friend on the head.

It's so hard
It's so high
It's how we try
to honor the sacrifices
    made by our dead.

A Prayer for the Place That Always Knew Me

Sorelle Weinstein

God,

I was a child when the pulse of this land first called to me, though I couldn't put it into words then. The rustling of the palm trees, like whispers of ancestors long gone, wrapped around my heart. I tasted Israel in chocolate milk from a bag, in pita from the *makolet*, in the scent of the air, and the warmth of the stone walls of the Kotel. There, I felt something shift in my chest. Not just the excitement of a new place, but something deep and quiet, like the first stirrings of a love I didn't yet know how to name. I walked those ancient streets, not knowing I was already walking a path set long before me, a journey I would one day claim as my own. The love for this land wasn't something I found; it was something that found me, pulling me close, even as a child.

And now, years later, I am still here, still bound to this land, still bound to You. God, It is a love story, isn't it? One that spans centuries, from the moment You first chose us, through the quiet moments of our wandering, and to this place, where our feet touch the soil our ancestors dreamed of. I didn't know that the decision to live here, to call this land my own, would mean feeling the weight of each life that was sacrificed to make this dream a reality.

I live here now, with my family, with my children who have grown up in this land. When our children, lions and lionesses, stand in uniform, they fight not just for their lives but for the life we've all chosen, for the life we've promised each other and to You. We are a people chosen for this land, but the price is high. The blood, the loss, the sacrifice — the price we pay for this life of purpose.

On Yom HaZikaron, when the sorrow is heavy in the air, when we remember each soldier and each victim of terror who gave their lives for the continuation of this land, we feel it all, deeply. Each of us knows someone who has fallen, someone who should still be here, still sharing this land with us. The grief is raw, a wound that feels like it cannot heal, a wound that has become part of who we are, part of the soul of this nation.

But even in the depth of grief, there is something else — something that rises to the surface: joy. When Yom HaAtzmaut comes, the grief doesn't vanish, but it transforms. We remember why we fight, why we endure. The streets, draped in blue and white, pulse with the rhythm of our hearts, unified in celebration, even as our hearts are heavy. The joy is not diminished by the sorrow; rather, it is made all the more precious. We know how fragile this existence is, how precarious it is to live a life of purpose in this land. We do not take it for granted. The sweetness of the day — of the people, the land, the future — is more vibrant because we know the cost of its existence.

It is the elasticity of the heart that allows us to carry both grief and joy, side by side. It stretches to accommodate the weight of our history, our dreams, and our fears. But it never breaks. It bends, it sways, but it does not snap.

God, our love for this land, for You, is deep and enduring. Even when the road is hard, when the pain is sharp, we remember why we're here. We remember that this love story, though full of sacrifice, is one we choose every day.

You gave us this land. You brought us back to the place where our ancestors once walked. And though the struggle is real, though the pain is heavy, we know this is where we belong. This land, this love, is ours. And we will continue to walk it, step by step, through the joy, through the grief, through the years, through the tears. This bond is unbreakable.

We recognize that this is just one chapter of our story. In the grand narrative of the Jewish people, this is one verse, one line of many. Yes, we are in the middle of it, amidst the sorrow, the loss, and the pain. But we also know that the next page will bring hope, will bring light.

We are writing this story as we live it, each of us playing a part, each of us contributing to the unfolding love story between the Jewish people and this land. The steps of our ancestors echo in the streets, and we walk in those footsteps. We feel the presence of the past with every loss, and yet, we are also writing the future. Our children will carry this story forward, and they will write new chapters, new verses, in the book of our people.

God, this is our love story. And though it is not always easy, we will continue to write it. Every day, every generation, every moment — one page at a time.

Ode to Quiet

Hila Bar

*Quiet implies a relatively low level of noise, while silence indicates an
    absence of sound altogether.*

To You who withdraws the quiet
And brings silence to my threshold
Let me reach out and draw it close
Wrap it around my ravaged soul,
And my body that aches for its cushion on the contours of my skin
For its viscous vapors to perform a billowing dance
For when we dance we pray,
And our movements ascend to Heaven.

What are you, silence, whose muteness lingers in the places that I go
Whose untainted purity seeps into my being
Rousing the soul and summoning its prayer
Stirring the spirit to sing sweet and clear
Probing the faith so deeply in the night
And beckoning the song from within.

What stroke of the brush do You streak across a nation?
To paint a picture of such grief
That hovers over a young soldier's grave;
To suffuse Your hue in a flame on the Day of Remembrance
With such fiery blaze;
Whose lunge of silence renders a nation breathless,
Until gasping for justice, for peace,
Understanding!
Some form of expression.

The first breath is released
In the primordial cry
Of a state being born:
We… hereby declare the establishment of a Jewish state in Eretz Yisrael,
to be known as the State of Israel.

A silence that bursts into a rhapsody of song
A bonfire of dance
Its frenzied flames whirling, leaping up to the sky
Souls ascending to heaven from their fiery storm
Soundlessly.
Look at the flames
How they dance,
And look at the warmth that they bring us.

How do You dwell among whispers of the ancient stone
That pulse across the plaza
Carrying through eons of eternity
The secrets of the deep
While letting the night give way to songs of the soul
Of unbroken faith
That defy the depths of the darkness.

And in the morning
When dawn shines her brilliant light
The rooster lifts his head and listens,
For in that fresh, cool light between night and day,
Where the embers lie parched,
The newborn has been soothed,
And the stones begin to soak up the sun,

Is the time that silence awakens the soul,
To draw the song from within.

And through the quiet of the air
A new day rings in
Amid the sweet, pure sounds of birdsong,
And ever so softly,
Gentle murmurings of the soul:
Lehagid ba-boker chasdekha

My song

Wildflowers | *Ronit Friedman*

A Twilight Prayer (towards Hallel)
Yael Sukenik

Our God, God of our fathers. Of Avraham and Yitzchak and Yaakov
God of our fathers who dwelled in Israel and Babylon and Rome, in
    Egypt and Morocco,
in Provence and Poland, who scattered us across all of the lands of the
    world.
Our God and God of our mothers, of Sarah and Rivka, Rachel and
    Leah
God of our mothers who dwelled in slavery and in exile and in
salvation, in the golden ages and the holocausts, in our land and across
    the world.
We stand before You in our land and with our land, tonight, among
    our people,
Hear my voice, God who gives heed to the voices that come before
    You.
In this year of 5785, in this place in the cycles of years between exile
    and redemption and the liminal space Your people sit now,
We tore our clothes and sat among our graves.
We come before You bereft
We tore our clothes and sat among our graves, our graves our
    everywhere – a stream in our consciousness and our feeds of
    the faces of our fallen
The rivers of Babylon where we wept are our rivers of tears that follow
    us haunted by those missing
in our cities, the faces of all those we have lost, the tears we stop to
    shed and the tears behind our eyes.
We call out from our depths with our voices and our tears.
Every year, we come before You to mourn our dead.
This year, we come before You, our hands empty
Our Father, our King, we stand for the sake of those we lost
our mothers and fathers, brothers and sisters, our children who fell
    living as Your people,

defending Your people – who died in Your name.

God of the fallen of wars and of cafes and buses and farms, of the fields
of war and the fields of dance and the fields of families,

of those who fell with guns in their hands and those who fell with
babies in their arms.

We cry out for them – that their blood be avenged, that their memory
be a blessing.

We implore You even as You care for their souls that You guide us in
the care of their memories and their families, in the care of their
people and the land that they loved.

In their names, we ask our salvation, the salvation of the people who
remember our covenant with our dead, as we remember our fathers'
covenant with You.

In their names, we ask You to answer us.

In their names, we ask for the courage to live in this moment You gave
us,

the moment of joy at everything we have yet to lose.

Our God who separates light from darkness and darkness from light,

night falls and we move from mourning to the joy we still carry in our
broken hearts.

Answer us, God of our fathers, of our mothers,

Answer us in these moments of twilights.

We stand before You tonight in and with our land, among and with
our people.

God of the land of Israel, of the people Israel,

God of time – who made the seventh day holy and ordered the months
with times of joy.

Who taught Your people, our sages, our leaders to do the same,

according to Your patterns of time and history.

Give us the courage to celebrate the land beneath our feet, even as we
fight to remain.

Give us the joy to celebrate the children in our arms without

forgetting the emptiness we still embrace of everything we have lost.

Grant us the presence to remember to take nothing for granted.

May the people You have commanded to complete Your praise not be
forgotten.

Halleluyah, we sing

Halleluyah, from the setting of this sun until its rising – may You who
gave us our children

remember us and them.

May we lift our cups in salvation, for today we are here, and we believe
we must, that You forget us not in freedom and not in chains.

God whose kindness is forever, the nations surround us as ever.

Perhaps we forgot that, but today we do not forget. You answered us,
we who read these words are free.

We beseech You that we all be free.

Let us live, let us proclaim You, Let us proclaim Your righteousness
that we seek to emulate.

Let us remind the nations blinded by hate and deceit that the nation of
Israel is created in the name of our just and righteous God.

This is the day You made – may our clouded joy well up in the miracle
of Your presence in our lives and the lives of Your people on
Your land.

Hoshiyah Na – save us, for we know You are with us.

You are forever. And we, Your people, rise up to sing Your praise – the
praise we sing in life.

The nation of Israel lives.

May the words of our mouths and the meditations of our hearts, our
cries of joy and of despair, the movements of our dance and our
arms in embrace and our tears shed in pain and in joy,

May they be acceptable to You, God, Rock and Redeemer of the
people Israel.

Yom HaAtzmaut

CELEBRATING ISRAEL'S
INDEPENDENCE AND STATEHOOD

A Prayer for Yom HaAtzmaut
The Editors

God on high,
Who makes dreamers believe in miracles.
Who breathes life into dry bones,
Whose dusty deserts bloom.
Who empowered David against Goliath.

Who could imagine a small nation,
Designed to survive millennia,
Of exile and Diaspora?
You watched over us,
We, who have returned to our ancient land,
Gifted to us
When we were just sand and stars.

Who else could have kept us
Searching, seeking, assembling,
Through the darkest generations –
Always hoping, praying,
That one day we could return home?

You have brought us back,
From the edges of death
From the blackness of oblivion,
To eat the sweet offerings of Your land,
To hear the cacophony of its shores,
To witness the gold of Your holy cities,
And the blush of Your perfect sunsets.

You have given the dreamers the tools to build,
The impulse to innovate,
The energy to create,
The dedication to redig our forefather's wells,
While we bring forth fresh water for the world.

Today we thank You,
For bringing us home,

We ask that You help us rebuild strong borders,
Keep our skies peaceful,
Bless Your people with silence while we sleep,
Laughter when we wake,
Sustenance for our livelihoods,
And transcendence for our souls.

May we celebrate Your presence among us,
May we see Your vision for the future of the people of Israel,
May we stay safe and satisfied, strong and serene,
Worthy of witnessing the final redemption, speedily in our days.

Soon in Our Days

Senai Guedalia, with Shira Lankin Sheps

This prayer is לעילוי נשמת *Yosef Malachi Guedalia Hy"d among all the soldiers who rose up to the* כיסא הכבוד, *the heavenly throne, on Simchat Torah, the first day of the Swords of Iron war.*

Dear God,
אבא שבשמים
(To our Father in Heaven)
Let our pain transform into purpose
Perhaps we don't know all the answers.

Please let us be content and happy
in our surrender to Your almighty power.

Hashem, we are in Your hands.
Thank You, God, for the gift of life,
for all the good You have blessed us with
and the souls You have given us and connected us with.

Blessed with the privilege of being conduits
for Your expression and will
for opening our eyes to see Your beauty,
opening our lips to speak Your praises,
and opening our hands to receive Your שפע (abundance).

Please, God, continue to allow us to live in Your land.
Send Your *Shechinah* to settle among us.
Let us live the realization of Your prophecies,
And bring to life Your Holy Land.

May the crops continue to grow
May the farmers live in peace to farm them.
May the markets thrive,
May every house have what they need.

May the brides and grooms circle each other,
Under Your *sukkat shelomekha,*
(Your sukkah of peace).
May the children learn,
With love in their hearts.

Protect our soldiers
and their families
in their endless dedication to You
and the land You have given us.

May You sit with the mourners of Zion,
May You heal the brokenhearted,
May You lift up Your people,
May we feel Your presence in our every moment.

Please, God, in complete faith, let the גאולה שלמה –
the complete redemption – come soon in our days.

The Marriage of Our People and Their Land | *Sefira Lightstone*

Flight to the Heavens

Ruti Eastman

Dear Father in Heaven,
We can be so grateful
for the way You guided Your Jewish people
in Israel
to place days of remembrance
before the day of celebration.

In Israel, our days of mourning the losses
that lead to independence
are nestled right up against the very independence they allowed.
In an almost dizzying emotional plunge
into the abyss
followed by an exhilarating flight to the heavens,
we observe our memorial days
just before our hard-won independence.

Thank You, Holy Father,
for structuring Your holy land
and Your Torah
in such a way as to teach us,
every day,
every year,
every moment,
to cope with this tumultuous world.

All Your teachings,
all Your timings,
help us to hug each other
during periods of collective pain,
to celebrate together
during moments of communal joy,
to find ways to light

and to improve the world
according to Your constant lessons.

Please continue to strengthen us
to remember that only together
may we be victorious.
Only together,
can we fulfill Your plan
of shining light to all the people
of Your precious world.

Guide us in being leading instruments
in Your glorious symphony
so that all will hold You in awe,
even at the ends of the earth.

A Prayer for the Future of Israel

Toby Klein Greenwald

To God above

I want to smell
Jasmine and fir trees
In my garden
I want to smell the forests and fountains of the north
The honeysuckle in our backyard

I want to feel
The Jerusalem winter chill
The cool stones of the Kotel
The gentle summer breeze when I sit beneath our pergola
On Shabbat
And the hot summer wind of the Negev

I want to feel
The soft and hard earth
Beneath my feet
As I wander
Through our wildflowers

I want to hear
The sound of children running up the pathway
Leading to our home, shouting
"Savta!"
(Grandma!)

I want to hear
The sound of the basketball pounding our neighbors' patio
And the yelp of their sons when they make a basket
Before they return to school
And to the army

I want to hear the sound of planes overhead
Protecting us

I want to see
Smiles, not stress, on faces in the street
Purple-red sunsets and snow
From our bay window
Overlooking the hills
Of Gush Etzion

And after a drought
Rainbows
That we prayed for
A sign of rain and that God
Will not destroy the world again
At least not that way
Though there are many kinds
Of floods

I want to see
Dew

I want to taste
The vegetable soup of my husband
A liberator of Jerusalem
Whose parents hid underground in Europe
The Moroccan fish of my son-in-law
Whose father wore a yellow star
at the age of seven in Tunisia
Blueberries from the Golan Heights
On the Syrian border
Cookies baked with love by my granddaughters
studying to be nurses;
Spicy BBQ meat with my old friends, who made aliyah
And who meet
Every Yom HaAtzmaut

I want to taste
The salt on my lips from the sea at the edge
Of Caesarea

I want to hear, once again, the ocean waves
Behind our daughter's chuppah
In Gush Katif

So many desires.
I want
A peaceful
Joyful
Tearless
Fearless
Land of Israel.

A Prayer of Thanksgiving for Immigrants on Independence Day in Israel

Yael Levine

Master of the Universe, we stand now before You,
impassioned and overflowing with gratitude, as we celebrate
Yom HaAtzmaut in the State of Israel.
We have already said in the morning services the
Hallel prayer, whose recitation was prescribed for this day.
We now deem it worthy to offer our own personal thanksgiving
      prayer for
the immense kindness You have shown us,
standing by our side and guiding us on our journey,
meriting us
to settle in the land of our
forefathers and foremothers.

For all these, we are eternally grateful to You.
"If our mouths were filled with song like the sea, our tongues with
      joy like its multitudes of waves,
and our lips with praise like the expanses of the heavens,
we could still not thank You and praise You enough, Lord our God
      and the God of our ancestors,
for all the goodnesses You have showered upon us."
There is no day more befitting than today
when the Jewish people gained their independence
after nearly two millennia,
to express the gratitude that fills our hearts, King of Kings,
for the opportunity to come and dwell in the State of Israel.
In doing so, we are partners in the fulfillment of the ideal
of returning to Zion and establishing a Jewish state
according to the Torah and vision of the prophets.
We are fortunate to carry out and realize the dream
of generations upon generations of Jews,
which, much to their sorrow, they were unable to realize.

We furthermore wish to express our appreciation to You, our

Creator,
for having implanted in us the very desire
and yearning
to ascend to the Holy Land.
How fortunate we are to have merited,
in the generation of the redemption
following the horrors of the Holocaust,
to partake in the process of the redemption,
and to contribute, as best we can,
to the development and enhancement of Israeli society
on a professional and personal level.

In coming to the Holy Land,
we seek to grow and to ascend spiritually.
We breathe in the air of this land, and feel its holiness in our
being.
Here in the land of our forefathers and foremothers,
we feel an even more profound connection to our nation,
and are grateful to live in alignment with our Jewish values.
Living here amongst our fellow Jewish brothers and sisters,
the words of the Psalmist, "Behold, how good and how pleasant it is
for brethren to dwell together in unity,"
resonate before our eyes.
Since settling in the State of Israel, we have encountered uplifting
      experiences,
and have witnessed the unique human fabric of Israeli society.

We beseech You to assist us in feeling at every moment of our
      being
the same aura of gratefulness regarding our aliyah and absorption,
even on hard days.
The transition to the State of Israel was and is yet
at times
accompanied by the need to adapt and acquire new ways of life.
Help us, Creator of the world, to rise above what we occasionally
consider to be challenges,
and observe the unequivocal positive aspects
inherent in residing here.

May it be Your will that as You have aided and sustained us thus
    far, so too,
You will continue to accompany and direct us
in the paths that are suited and right for us.
Protect all our family members as the pupil of an eye,
and grant success to our offspring.

The State of Israel has undergone from its inception until the
    present
day, without cease and without respite, threats from without by our
enemies who have risen up against us to destroy us. Defend us,
guard
Your people Israel, and may the approaching footsteps of the
    Messiah
be speedily heard in the streets of Jerusalem and throughout the
    State
of Israel. And rebuild Your Temple, as at the beginning, and
    establish
Your sanctuary upon its foundation, and let us witness its
    rebuilding and
elate us by its restoration. Amen, so may it be Your will.

Homeland Calling | *Yael Harris Resnick*

A Prayer for Small Things
(or, Aliyah in Wartime)

Tamar Ron Marvin

Ribbono Shel Olam—
I turn to You
Almost paralyzed by the insignificance of my needs.

But You have, in Your wisdom and kindness, interlaced our moments
with prayers for the small things:
for the sun rising, again;
for a bite of bread;
for using the bathroom.

I need to ask You for other small things, things that need new
    attention as we settle in our homeland.
I need to ask for internet access — *quick,* before the kids complain.
For our coffeemaker to finally arrive.
For the cat to forgive us for making her travel on that plane.

We made the big move, the important changes, the monumental
    decision
With confidence in Your ways,
With faith that You are there in the monumental.
For this is a prayer for *Eretz Yisrael.*
And we made this move "by the grace of God."

But now I turn to You for the smallness of things.
I thank You for the smallest of joys.
Thank You for helping us in the small ways
that will make this land our home.
And as we immerse in the dailiness of our lives…

The small things are part of our journey to take root here. They ease
    our destiny in this beautiful, holy land. Your land.

Recognizing those small things in prayer interlaces our days with Your wisdom and kindness.

Because those small things connect. They flow into larger things, into the most important things.

Every life traverses the daily grind, despite my best preferences for, instead, the abstract, the visionary, the conceptual. Yet Torah lives in the rise and fall of a day.

Help me remember.

Please fulfill the needs, big and small, of Your nation, hostages still in Gaza or back at home, families separated by war, the widows and orphans, soldiers on the front, volunteers in the field, the wounded in recovery.

May it be Your will that I open myself to You — through the smallness of my needs.

Please open Your hands and satisfy all the needs of all of us, according to Your will.

Independence

Alana Ruben

"Gotenyu!!" – !גאטעניו
My grandmother said in grief-strained Yiddish,
when unholy fates befell our family or our people.
"Be independent!" she demanded of me.
Life demanded of me.
I have grown my independence in this land.
Seeded myself, on behalf of my grandchildren,
between the crevices of hard Jerusalem stone.

Could these be anything else but the Days of Revelation?
A time of war not over land, but over Your very existence.

Our God, God of All the Worlds,
Today, on Independence Day, we stand before You,
like sands on the seashore —
The liminal material that holds the world together —
Binding the dry land to the seas;
order to chaos;
the known to the unknown;
the holy to the unholy.

Throughout history, alternating waves —
Waves of dreams and construction,
waves of demons and destruction —
pounded upon Your people,
changing slightly our form,
but never our essence.

Today, on Independence Day, we stand before You as warriors against
all the monsters that have risen to destroy knowledge of You
and Your ways.

Today, on Independence Day, we stand before You, like stars in the

heavens, each one of us a fusion of energy, constellated by Your will, to
guide those seeking earthly justice, eternal truths, and the ways of
      peace.

Today, we stand before You, a more mature nation, no longer the
      Children of Israel.

Overnight, we became the Parents of Israel, guardians to all our
nations' children, and guardians to what remains of Good in Your
      World.

The near-constant sunshine makes the boundaries of our identity,
      our reality,
        our sanity so clear.
Help us to steadfastly carve more deeply our paths home
—through this modern wilderness,
From wherever we may stand.

Are we not all obligated by our grandmothers and our progeny to
      "build our independence"?

Eternal light without end, *Ohr Ain Sof,*
Bring us, with gentleness and patience, into alignment with Your
      being and teachings,
so that we are able to complete the mission passed down to us by our
      nation's founders,
to realize Israel's greatest potentials and promise;
and to dance fearlessly at daybreak once again.

Fly Free | *Micol Bayer*

A Prayer for the Redemption of Israel

Chana Tannenbaum

A song of ascents.

שִׁיר הַמַּעֲלוֹת בְּשׁוּב ה' אֶת־שִׁיבַת צִיּוֹן הָיִינוּ כְּחֹלְמִים:

When the Lord restores the fortunes of Zion —we see it as in a dream.
   (Psalms 126:1)

On the day when…
The people who walked in darkness
Have seen a brilliant light;
Upon those who dwelt in a land of gloom,
Light has dawned. (Isaiah 9:1)

Hear my cry, O God,
Heed my prayer. (Psalms 61:2)

Lord, our God, Rock of Israel, we turn to You in these trying times,
crying out for Your mercy and redemption.
Our land is in turmoil, our people suffer from war, terror, and
      uncertainty.
Families have been torn apart, hostages remain in captivity, and
innocent lives have been lost.

My children have gone forth from Me
And are no more. (Jeremiah 10:18)

They had taken the women captive…
…carried them off and went their way. (from Samuel I, 30:2)

For these things do I weep,
My eyes flow with tears. (Lamentations 1:16)

Lord, see the suffering of Your people,
the innocent blood spilled,
the cries of the orphans and widows.

Even in this darkness, we know that You have not forsaken us.
Though Your face is hidden.

You are indeed a God who hides in concealment,
O God of Israel, who brings victory! (Isaiah 45:15)

Be strong and resolute, I remind myself.
Be not in fear or in dread of them;
for it is indeed your God who marches with you:
He will not fail you or forsake you. (Deuteronomy 31:6)

We rejoice in Your promise
That You will not reject us or spurn us so as to destroy us
That You will not annul Your covenant with us:
for You are our God. (from Leviticus 26:44)

We see Your miracles unfold before our eyes.
You have shielded us from destruction,
protected us from missiles,
and saved us from bus bombings and terror.

מֵאֵת ה' הָיְתָה זֹּאת הִיא נִפְלָאת בְּעֵינֵינוּ:

This is the Lord's doing;
It is marvelous in our sight. (Psalms 118:3)

Lord, we long for the day when peace will fill our land.

וְשַׁבְתִּי אֶת־שְׁבוּת עַמִּי יִשְׂרָאֵל וּבָנוּ עָרִים נְשַׁמּוֹת וְיָשָׁבוּ וְנָטְעוּ כְרָמִים וְשָׁתוּ
אֶת־יֵינָם וְעָשׂוּ גַנּוֹת וְאָכְלוּ אֶת־פְּרִיהֶם:

We trust in Your promise:
That You will restore Your people Israel.
They shall rebuild ruined cities and inhabit them;
They shall plant vineyards and drink their wine;
They shall till gardens and eat their fruits. (from Amos 9:14)

And the desolate land, after lying waste in the sight of every passerby,
shall again be tilled. (Ezekiel 36:34)

We pray that the redemption continues,
and that all who remain in exile are gathered home.

וְלָקַחְתִּי אֶתְכֶם מִן־הַגּוֹיִם וְקִבַּצְתִּי אֶתְכֶם מִכָּל־הָאֲרָצוֹת
וְהֵבֵאתִי אֶתְכֶם אֶל־אַדְמַתְכֶם:

For You have said:
"I will take you from among the nations
and gather you from all the countries,
and I will bring you back to your own land." (Ezekiel 36:24)

The land flourishes, yet we yearn for complete security.

They shall build houses and dwell in them,
They shall plant vineyards and enjoy their fruit. (Isaiah 65:21)

Cities that were destroyed long ago are now vibrant again.
Cities that are now destroyed will be made vibrant again.

For, God, You have rebuilt the ravaged places,
and replanted the desolate land.
God, You have spoken and will act. (from Ezekiel 36:38)

Yet, there is mourning among us.
Too many have been lost, too many tears have been shed.
We plead with You to turn our sorrow into joy.

הָפַכְתָּ מִסְפְּדִי לְמָחוֹל לִי פִּתַּחְתָּ שַׂקִּי וַתְּאַזְּרֵנִי שִׂמְחָה:

You turned my lament into dancing,
You undid my sackcloth and girded me with joy. (Psalms 3:12)

הַזֹּרְעִים בְּדִמְעָה בְּרִנָּה יִקְצֹרוּ:

They who sow in tears
shall reap with songs of joy. (Psalms 126:5)

And may the streets of Jerusalem once again
echo with the laughter of children.
And the squares of the city shall be crowded

with boys and girls playing in the squares. (Zechariah 8:5)

We ask also for renewal.
Give us new strength, as You have said:
"And I will give you a new heart and put a new spirit into you:
I will remove the heart of stone from your body
and give you a heart of flesh;
And I will put My spirit into you…." (Ezekiel 36:26-27)

And we will continually renew our relationship with You.

Help us, O God, our Deliverer,
for the sake of the glory of Your name. (Psalms 79:9)

We trust in Your promise:

וְאָמַר בַּיֹּום הַהוּא הִנֵּה אֱ-לֹהֵינוּ זֶה קִוִּינוּ לֹו וְיֹושִׁיעֵנוּ
זֶה ה' קִוִּינוּ לֹו נָגִילָה וְנִשְׂמְחָה בִּישׁוּעָתֹו:

In that day they shall say:
This is our God;
We trusted in the One who delivered us.
This is God, in whom we trusted;
Let us rejoice and exult in God's deliverance! (Isaiah 25:9)

Amen.

Lag BaOmer

A Prayer for Lag BaOmer
The Editors

Dear God of Compassion, Grace, Mercy, and Truth:

On this day, as we remember that You stopped the ancient plague
that You had inflicted on Rabbi Akiva's students,
when they turned away from each other in arrogance,
when they refused each other the honor they each were due,
we pause to mourn them and learn from them.

We mourn their loss and we learn from them
the power of sharing in "*kinat sofrim,*"
the joy of debate in the name of the truth of Torah,
the reward of doing battle together in the *beit midrash*
for the glory of Torah and its resolutions and its open questions –
and not on the battlefield, where there is no glory in loss.

During this somber season,
we remember the oppressors who sought
to snuff out the Torah of Rabbi Akiva
and that of Rabbi Shimon bar Yochai,
and rejoice in their teachings that have accompanied
      the Jewish people
through the two thousand years since.

May the bonfires we ignite to commemorate those of yore illuminate
      our way
as we bring the fire of Torah and the light of tradition to our future
      generations,
with passion for truth, compassion for each other, and respect for Your
      ways of peace.

A Prayer for Achvah and Ahavat Yisrael

Togetherness and Love of Israel
(based on the prayer of Rabbi Eliezer in BT Berakhot 16b)

Karen Miller Jackson

יְהִי רָצוֹן מִלְּפָנֶיךָ ה' אֱלֹקֵינוּ, שֶׁתְּשַׁכֵּן בְּפוּרֵינוּ –
אַהֲבָה וְאַחְוָה וְשָׁלוֹם וְרֵיעוּת.

May it be Your will, Lord our God, to cause us to dwell in our lot –
love and brotherhood, peace and friendship.

Like we wish a groom and bride under the *chuppah*

אַהֲבָה וְאַחְוָה וְשָׁלוֹם וְרֵיעוּת.

May *Am Yisrael* find ways to dwell in
Respect, acceptance, shared commitment and harmony

Between
Religious and secular
Right and the left
Sephardim and Ashkenazim
Jews of Israel and the Diaspora
Jews and the nations

To love your fellow Jew like yourself – to do small acts to increase
feelings of kinship and community among *Am Yisrael*.

May it be Your will, Lord our God, to cause our leaders to find ways to
model these values.

Like Aaron the high priest, who was called *ohev shalom* (lover of
peace) and *rodef shalom* (pursuer of peace),
who ran to find ways to make amends.

וְתַרְבֶּה גְבוּלֵנוּ בְּתַלְמִידִים וְתַצְלִיחַ סוֹפֵנוּ אַחֲרִית וְתִקְוָה.

And may You make our borders rich in disciples
and cause us ultimately to succeed, so that we have a good end and hope.

May our borders be filled again with the sounds of joy and life, of farming and praying, and dancing and protecting.

May our borders be rich with children learning and playing, and may all who live on our borders live long lives and be sources of strength and hope.

וְתָשִׂים חֶלְקֵנוּ בְּגַן עֵדֶן, וְתַקְנֵנוּ בְּחָבֵר טוֹב וְיֵצֶר טוֹב בְּעוֹלָמֶךְ.

And may You set our portion in the Garden of Eden,
and may You establish for us a good friend
and a good inclination in Your world.

A good friend –
May we find ways to be a good friend and good neighbor,
to be an *ohev Yisrael,* one who loves Israel.

A good inclination –
May we find ways to develop a good eye
and view others in the best light.

May we find ways to develop a good ear and learn to hear the goodness in what others say.

May we find ways to build each other up
and not tear each other down.

וְנַשְׁכִּים וְנִמְצָא יְחוּל לְבָבֵנוּ לְיִרְאָה אֶת שְׁמֶךָ,
וְתָבֹא לְפָנֶיךָ קוֹרַת נַפְשֵׁנוּ לְטוֹבָה.

And may we rise early and find the aspiration of our hearts to fear Your
name, and may the satisfaction of our souls come before You, for the best.

May we wake up to a peaceful land, from within and without
May our hearts be filled with humility and aspiration
May our souls be filled with healing and satisfaction
May our words and actions come before You, God, for the best.

Flickers from Another World

Shira Lankin Sheps

God,
I am looking for You amongst the flames
The shadows are flaring up, higher
Reflecting a release of darkness,
swallowed up by light.

My eyes burn as I watch
Smoke tendrils skimming my skin
Wind scented like mystery
I am searching for Your secrets.

Have the mystics buried the answers
In the towering bonfires?
Do the truths pop up on every hilltop
In fires of miracles?

The skies are filled with sparks
That escaped the wild dancing,
Flickers of another world,
That we can only see tonight.

God, I am searching in the blaze
For the hidden meanings,
The holy pathways,
The revelation that we are all waiting for…

Tonight, we can taste it,
A small serving of the beyond,
Elusive and everlasting,
While we search for the spiritual in the mundane.

Birkat HaHamah: The Blessing for the Sun | *Sheva Chaya Shaiman*

In the Cave of My Soul

Rachel Sharansky Danziger

In the cave of my soul
all is well-ordered.
The altar stands just so.
The candles burn brightly.
The angels sing and their harmonies run smoothly,
one into the other,
intricate and true.

But You have not made us to be cave-dwellers, God.
You have not formed us for the unchallenged quietude
of our private spaces.

Go forth,
You said.
Go forth.

Go forth and leave the cave behind.
The ark behind.
The enclosed spaces of our interiority behind.
The clean place where the soul can sing, uninterrupted.

Go forth into the messy world that lies between
one person and another.
Go forth into the place where our songs and visions clash.
Go forth into the place where one heart's edges
can sometimes cut another.
Go forth into a place that can be loud and harsh.
In that place,
where the light we carry sputters,
challenged by the light in other people's hands,
lies the fertile ground —
The battleground —
Where we can sow —

Or struggle,
where deeper understanding can take root,
Or we can burn the whole world down.

God,
as we heed Your call
and step beyond our inner caves,
grant us compassion.
Grant us the strength to see that
which we don't agree with,
and respond with caring.
Grant us the patience to ask questions
instead of yelling answers in each other's faces.
Grant us the inner calm to explore and not reject,
to open doors instead of shutting them.
Let our eyes see the good in our brothers, our sisters,
instead of scorching all the world with scorn.

May we sow seeds of understanding and collaboration
in all this fertile ground that lies between us,
And may we remember, always,
that this messy space
is our field
to tend to
And to guard.

May we stand rooted and strong
against those who work for our destruction,
And may our roots
Be ever
Intertwined.

Yom Yerushalayim

MARKING JERUSALEM'S
REUNIFICATION IN 1967

A Prayer for Yom Yerushalayim

The Editors

Dear God of Unity and Oneness,
On this day, we express our thanksgiving for Your blessings
in saving the Jewish people and the Jewish state
from the mighty armies that surrounded them in war,
with speed, conviction, and Your outstretched arm,
and we celebrate Your bounty in providing
for the reunification of Jerusalem,
Your holy city,
Our succor through the ages.

Please continue to wrap Jerusalem in Your light,
that it may reflect off the Jerusalem stone of
both old and new construction,
and remind us to insist on forging our paths in this city of peace.

May it be so, and may we merit to participate
in the rebuilding of the redeemed Jerusalem,
and to live up to the model You have established us to be,
a light unto the nations,
which goes forth from Zion,
a home of peace and prayers for all nations.

A Prayer for Jerusalem

Tzipora Lifchitz

Jerusalem, she glows — dust-covered, but never dulled.
     A queen in a headscarf, wrapped in time,
      holy breath tangled in human sighs.

God, You are everywhere, but here — most.

She hums with voices caught between stone and sky,
prayers pressed into cracks, hearts breaking open in longing and faith.

She hears her name from the world over, promising to be home:
Next year, Next year.

She smells of fresh pita, of cracked *siddurim* (prayerbooks), and the
     electricity of pending redemption.

She sees palms stretched open. For coins. For bread. For blessing.

She moves — zigzagged between scooters and strollers,
     lined with bumper stickers in rhyming Kabbalah,
     jumping ropes in children's hands,
     tzitzit swinging against the gun holsters of men.

Women carry *Tehillim* (Psalms), groceries, babies, ideas, innovation,
     the weight of their grandmothers' prayers,
     and of the world they want to build.

Teens lose themselves, find themselves, lose themselves again,
     just as they have on these hills, these winding alleyways,
     and these caves, since time before time.

Jerusalem is ageless. Modern. Layered. Complicated.
Prying — but only because she loves deeply.

She is peace surrounded by tension.
Holiness tangled in hurry.

Eternity pulsing through the ordinary.

And in times of loss, we cry.
But there is no place I would rather cry than Jerusalem.
          Here, the *Shechinah* weeps, too.

Living in Jerusalem is a living miracle,
and it takes constant work to live in the magic.

Traffic jams, winding around the City of David.
          Taxi drivers mutter psalms,
          weaving in between meetings scheduled,
          late appointments for the manicurist,
          between the Kotel and carpool.

Here, the mundane and the sacred are one breath, one heartbeat,
          one slow inhale of blessing.

The Jerusalem grocer is a *kohen*, my children's heads beneath his
          hands, "May *Hashem* bless you and grant you peace."

I've carried pockets full of prayer slips,
          folded dollar bills from distant hands, through security,
          through stopovers, through time, to bring them home.

I've signed my name alongside my city's name — With love, with
          longing, from Jerusalem.

All turn towards Jerusalem to pray.

Though history feels like an endless night, the prophecy of Jerusalem
          stands on the edge of dawn.

Step through her gates, behold gold and honey.
Her faces are photos faded, and photos waiting to be taken,
          stories turned fables and stories waiting to unfold:

Darkness cracks open. The blazing sun shatters her into morning.

She carries many flames, a city of fire.

And what do we see in the flames?
>They say that in the Redemption, we will see You everywhere.
>In every blade of grass, in every stone, in the eyes of a stranger,
>in the concrete beneath our feet.

Your glory will be as plain as the ocean, as abundant as the tide.

But even now, if I close my eyes, still my breath,
>face inward — toward my own Jerusalem, I'll hear it.

A flicker

This soul within me, I am holy.

Kadosh. Kadosh. Kadosh.

The entire earth, from the ordinary to the Divine,
is filled with Your glory.

May we see it as plainly as waters cover the sea.

Birkat HaKohanim: Blessing of the Priests | *Avigail Wieder*

A New Song of Zion

Avital Macales

We drive into Jerusalem every day.
I'm not sure which one of us is in the driver's seat, You or I.

Every time we pass the road sign that points toward Jerusalem,
I wonder how I merited to live in my ancestors' dream,
to be counted in the unfolding of an ancient promise.

By the rivers of Babylon,
there we sat,
and wept,
as we remembered Zion.

On the road this morning from Gush Etzion to Jerusalem,
Waze announces:
"Traffic building up ahead. Ten minutes added."
Oof. I'm going to be late for work.

Then I think of my ancestors' GPS —
God's Plan Spoken —
offering them its most devastating recalculation yet:
"*It will take hundreds, if not thousands, of years*
till you see the city you were
so brutally
torn away from."

OK, OK.
I think I can handle this delay.

I look up ahead —
dozens of cars are trying to get through the checkpoint
at the same time,
all wishing to
get to Zion
as well.

There, on the willows,
we hung up our lyres,
for our captors asked us there for songs,
our tormentors for amusement:
"Sing us one of the songs of Zion!"
How can we sing the Lord's song
in a foreign land?!

Traffic comes to a standstill,
and I press the brake.
I sit with my ancestors by the rivers,
and wait with them in their silence,
stuck.
God, how could they not sing?
I wonder.
What is left of an exiled people,
if not their music?
Their voice?

I begin to hum.

A loud honk jolts me from behind —
"Hey, *Geveret*, it's time to move forward!"
A whisper from among the willows says—
Yes, go on,
sing us a new song of Zion.
You can.

A song of ascents.
When the Lord restores the exiles of Zion, we shall be like dreamers.

I drive through the checkpoint,
wave to the soldiers,
and thank them
for playing their part
in making this dream come true.

Up ahead, the tunnels await me —
the last, long stretch
before we get to the city of longing.

Somewhere within me,
I remember my first steps toward Zion —
a toddler at JFK airport,
my right hand holding my mother's,
and the other clutching a bag of Cheerios.

My father counts the suitcases one last time
before they disappear down the conveyor belt.
Then he counts my two older sisters and me
(I'm wearing a red t-shirt that says "I'm third")
and finally, he leads us to the gate —
the gateway for weepers,
dreamers,
singers whose lyres — no longer left hanging —
have been sent down the conveyor belt as well.

Then our mouths will be filled with laughter,
and our tongues with songs of praise.

My mother says I cried during takeoff.
It may be because I was out of Cheerios.
Or it might be because,
sometimes,
it can be frightening
to live in the time of redemption.

I enter the tunnels,
and suddenly —

You still there?

Everything is dark.
So dark
and long,

with unexpected bends,
the end nowhere in sight.

Waze gives up as well.

Are we still on our way to Jerusalem?

My dear exiled river-sitters,
now I see what it feels like
when despair drives you

to stop
singing.

One last curve of the road,
and suddenly — light!
Zion unfolding before us!

I exit the tunnels with a sigh with relief, but also wonder —
did we really have to go this way?
God's Plan has *Spoken*, but…
mind if I check the navigation settings You're using?

Then among the nations they will say—
God has done great things for them!

The hum of life through the streets of Jerusalem
swirls around us,
with children laughing,
and elders sitting and chatting —
and I see that, yes,

You have done great things for us.

And though the road still stretches ahead,
I hear something stirring —
lyres, released, strumming freely in the breeze,
playing a new song of Zion.

So we will play. We will sing. We will rejoice.

Gateway | *Ronit Friedman*

A Prayer for Jerusalem, Born of the Deep
Sarah Tuttle-Singer

God of the beating heart of Jerusalem,
Source of her breath and being,
You who formed her hills from the ancient sea,
Who set her foundations in the bones of the earliest life,
Who carved her valleys with the memory of water—
I call to You now.

For before there were stones, there was sea,
Before there were walls, there were waves,
Before there were battlements, there was only the deep.

Jerusalem rose from the waters You gave and withdrew, and still that
        sea remains, hidden in her bones.
In the limestone that once cradled shells,
in the fossils pressed into desert rock,
in the hush before the rain when the air tastes of salt.

The tides abide.

God of the depths and the heights,
God of the wellspring and the wilderness,
Help us remember:
Jerusalem was first a place of gathering —
Not of dividing.
A place where waters mingled —
Not where blood was spilled.
A place where the great currents of the deep
Moved together in harmony,
As we, too, must learn to be carried and moved.

For even now, the sea is in us.
It is in the thrum of the market,
In the rise and fall of voices in the shuk,

In the shifting tide of feet on stone,
In the rhythm of prayer, of argument, of song.
It is in the spice merchant measuring zaatar and rose petals,
The weaver tying knots into fabric,
The map seller tracing his finger along the roads that have carried
    generations home,
for here we are.

God of the first waters,
God of the rivers that remember their way back to the sea,
Gather us together as You once gathered the depths.
Let us meet as the currents meet,
not in conquest,
but in the knowing that we are of the same source.

Infinite You.

For we are the children of this city's dust and water,
of its sorrow and its splendor,
of its history and its hope.
We are the shopkeeper handing warm bread to the hungry,
the artist who gathers shattered glass
and makes it whole again with molten gold,
the teacher who helps the lost child find the thread of meaning
in the words.
We are the mother pressing her palm to the Western Wall,
And the father waiting at the bus stop, looking for his son's face.
We are the student on the train,
reading scripture beside the soldier who dozes,
beside the grandmother who hums an old song,
beside the dreamer who has journeyed a lifetime
just to be in this place.

God of the deep past,
God of the future ever flowing,
Teach us to remember what came before
So we do not drown in what we have built.

Remind us that the walls are not what make Jerusalem —
It is the water that still moves beneath them,
It is the people who carry her story,
It is You, the beating heart of this city,
Still pulsing beneath our feet.

Let us listen through our seashells ears.
Let us hear the hidden waves,
The echo of the sea within the stone,
And within each other.
And let that be what draws us together —
Not fear, not fire, not war,
But the knowledge that once,
Before all this,
We were all part of the same sea.

And if we listen, if we look,
Perhaps we will remember how to move as one again, together.

Amen.

A Tefillah for a Complete Yerushalayim

Rachel Berko

Ribbono Shel Olam,

My Father, Master, and Redeemer,
Only You know when we will see and feel a complete *Yerushalayim*.
Only You know when Your third and final home will be rebuilt.
Only You, *Hashem*, can give us glimpses of hope and gems along our
      journey toward completion.

Do I do my part to speed up this process?
Do I yearn for this truly wondrous moment?
Do I have faith that *Mashiach's* announcement will be soon?
Do I pray to feel even a glimpse of what a complete *Yerushalayim* will
      be like?

I can only hope,
I can only imagine,
I can only dream
Of the bursting happiness and light we will feel
At seeing the *Beit HaMikdash* standing.

I pray *Hashem's* love will be more clear,
Our judgment will fade away,
Our tears will be joyous,
Oh, how I yearn for this day!

May we feel this process of complete redemption
Unfold before our eyes.
May we look up one day
And see the sun of *Yerushalayim* truly rise.

Sacred Horizon | *Leah Luria*

HaMakom (The Place)

Dina Guedalia, mother of Yosef Malachi Guedalia Hy"d

HaMakom, Your glory is apparent,
We bring ourselves fully to You,
With grace, faith, and certainty,

"ה' מלך ה' מלך ה' ימלוך לעולם ועד" (שמות ט"ו: י"ח)

The Lord will reign to all eternity.

Our story shines,

"כלבנת הספיר" (שמות כ"ד: י')

(like the forming of a sapphire brick)
Our love and longing
turn to song and praise,

"תבואי תשורי מראש אמנה" (שיר השירים ד': ח')

(Shall you come, you shall look from the peak of Amanah (faith))

Yerushalayim!
יראה ושלמות
(awe and perfection)
אש ומים
(fire and water)
The fires of destruction transform into fires of yearning,
The waters of the flood become soft-flowing and timeless,
מים חיים
(living waters)
nourishing our lives, sustaining and strengthening our connections,

"כמה כוח יש לנו" (מיומנו של יוסף מלאכי גדליה הי"ד)

How powerful we are (from the journal of Yosef Malachi Guedalia,
Hy"d)
We are *Yerushalayim*,
Radiating gentleness with strength,
Modesty with leadership,
Truth and kindness, with justice.

In synchronicity, we sing

"עוד יוסף חי" (בראשית מ"ה: כ"ו)

(Joseph is still alive)
in harmony with Serach Bat Asher
entering a place of peace
Weaving tears and song together,

"למען שמו באהבה" (סידור, עמידה)

(For the sake of His Name, with love)
For you, *Yerushalayim*

"המקום אשר יבחר" (דברים י"ב: ה')

(the place which the Lord your God shall choose)
We choose life
I forever am "אם הבנים שמחה"

(תהילים קי"ג: ט')

(as a happy mother of children)
I am prayer itself
Walking in unison as one with You towards all You encompass,
Being present, bringing forth the redemption
with higher consciousness,
We have the ability to transmute pain and carry it as love
We can create order from chaos
Let us perceive the world with "Eyes of Jerusalem"
As we emerge and see so much more,
knowing good, becoming pure joy!

"ופרוש עלינו סוכת שלומיך" (סידור, ברכת השכיבנו)

And spread over us the shelter of mercy, life, and peace
ברחמים
(in mercy)

The Lion's Gate | *Leah Jacobson*

Yerushalayim: Above and Below

Rachel Sharansky Danziger

Hashem

For so long we have walked through dry deserts,
and the dream of this place
lent strength to our feet.

Yerushalayim, we thought,
in Ethiopia and Russia
in too many places
too many seasons
of hardship and loss.
Yerushalayim, we thought,
and our feet grew lighter,
our hearts more resolved.

When walls and hatred closed on us
we looked to this dream
to open up the narrow spaces
of distress
Inside our soul.

Yerushalayim, we thought,
and the horizon grew broader.
Yerushalayim, we thought,
and found the courage to stand up.

The prayers and dreams of countless generations
lapped upon the shores of the *Yerushalayim* in our minds
And we were like dreamers cast into reality
when our feet found their way
To *Yerushalayim shel Mata*, earthly Jerusalem,
which exists outside of dreams.
A place of stone and dust and olives.

A place where we can taste eternity
even as our feet our rooted in the ground.
Where we can touch a wall and feel the thrum of history,
a beating heart inside a city,
an ancient swelling song.

Hashem, we rejoice in this privilege,
The privilege of touching where our ancestors could but dream.
And we are grateful, so deeply grateful,
for the dream of *Yerushalayim* that gave them comfort
and lent them purpose, patience, strength.

Thank You, *Hashem*, for the lighthouse that shone
Out of the idea of *Yerushalayim*
And for the light of physical *Yerushalayim*
which we are fortunate enough to feel
Upon our faces.

Vibrant Jerusalem

Anne Gordon

My landmarks of Jerusalem were gone.
Not destroyed, but built up and around and over.
A wasteland of field was now
Many classy, four-story Jerusalem stone apartment buildings.
An expansion of the city.

I never encountered a barren, withered Jerusalem.
The holy city has always been a bouncy, noisy, jumbled, hectic place,
punctuated by pockets of serenity.

Views of the Old City and the Judean Hills,
with a sky that seems touchable.
A nearly tangible reminder of You, who are there for us all.

The privilege is ours, with gratitude to You.
And to the paratroopers, their shofar, their famous upturned faces.
A proclamation: The Kotel is in our hands,
Returned to our hands.
The Jordanian border never ran through Jerusalem for me.
Thank You.
Can we barter in the Arab shuk
On our way to the Cardo?
We'll wander the Jewish Quarter,
Meander down to the Western Wall, that holy retaining wall of
Judaism's ancient Temples.
We spread our local wings,
and know we can't take these boons for granted.
But almost, we do. That's the privilege. Living in the mix.

A mix of ancient with the newest of new;
Intensity embodied,
with frustration and passion running hand in hand,
from the muezzin to car horns to babies caterwauling to the non-stop

      drilling
that renews the modern city.
A desolate Jerusalem seems laughable –
like those foxes that once confirmed its desolation (Makkot 24).

The Jerusalem I know is a city of yearning –
the site of dreams sparked and embraced and fulfilled.
Jerusalem stone playing host to those who brought their wishes
to the heart of a land, a people, a city surrounded by hills.
An eternal holiness that sheds light on what matters most.

It's the roots of thousands of years of heritage,
The place we were promised to inherit
An ingathering of diverse exiles
the family that we were always a part of, but often distant from,
until Jerusalem. To where we come home,
the instinctive belonging in the place that we, the Jewish people
triumph in the face of everything else.

The prophet Zechariah foretells Your return to the "city of truth,"
and the return of the very elderly to the city's squares (8:3–4),
representatives of peace, who cannot go out to war –
and Rabbi Akiva's reassurance for a rebuilt city.
The foundations of a place for You to dwell –
we dwell with You.

It's the birthday parties in the parks,
the parades that mark special occasions,
the chatter and yelling and laughter and music
of family life shed from one apartment to the next.

Jerusalem offers the past and the future.
With vibrancy that keeps it going,
Roots in antiquity,
Reach in modernity,
and growth by Your will,
surrounded by the echoes of prophecy.

About the Editors

Shira Lankin Sheps, MSW, is a writer, editor, workshop facilitator, and clinically-trained therapist. She founded and published *The Layers Project Magazine,* an online magazine that explored the challenges and triumphs of the lives of Jewish women, and is the author of *LAYERS: Personal Narratives of Struggle, Resilience, & Growth of Jewish Women* (Toby Press, an imprint of Koren, 2021). Shira's essays and articles have been published by *The Times of Israel, JTA, The Jewish Press, Kveller, The Forward, The Jewish Link, The Jerusalem Post, World Mizrachi,* and of course, *The Layers Project.* She earned a BA in English Literature at Stern College of Yeshiva University and a Masters of Social Work from the Silberman School of Social Work at Hunter College. She lives in Jerusalem with her husband and children. She is a co-editor of the Az Nashir series. Shira is the executive director and founder of The SHVILLI Center, and publisher of The Layers Press.

Rabbanit Anne Gordon is the deputy editor of Ops & Blogs at *The Times of Israel.* A veteran educator, Anne lives in Jerusalem with her family, where she co-hosts both the daily podcast, "Talking Talmud," and "The Chochmat Nashim Podcast," as co-founder of the organization. She is a graduate of Drisha Institute's Scholars Circle and holds a BA in History & Philosophy, an MA in Judaic Studies from Harvard University, and is ABD in her pursuit of a PhD in Jewish Education. She is a co-editor of the Az Nashir series. A Sefaria Word-by-Word fellow, Anne is currently writing on the interplay between biblical and rabbinic literature, a study in the Book of Proverbs.

Rachel Sharansky Danziger is a Jerusalem-born writer and educator who writes about the intersections between daily life, Tanach, and the art of storytelling. Having researched personal narratives of religious transformation for her MA in American History, she continues to explore questions of faith, emotions, and community formation in Jewish texts. Her work can be found in *The Times of Israel, Tablet Magazine, Kveller,* and other online venues. Rachel teaches Tanach at Matan, Pardes, Maayan, and Torah-in-Motion. She is a co-editor of the Az Nashir series. She is a SHVILLI educator and a Sefaria Word-by-Word fellow, where she is writing on family drama in the biblical book of Judges.

Writers

Alana Ruben is an Israeli/Canadian/American writer and theater artist who lives and creates in Israel, most recently "Esther's Throne" and "Esther Dresses in Divinity" (Jerusalem Biennale 2023/24). Israel, in all its expressions, is and eternally will be the great love of her soul.

Avital Macales happily lives in Efrat, just twenty minutes from Jerusalem (on a good day). Armed with a BA and MA in Hebrew Language, she spends her days geeking out as a Hebrew copyeditor and her nights bringing stories to life through music and theater. A singer, songwriter, actress, and playwright, Avital has co-written four original musicals — "Count the Stars: The Journey of Avraham & Sara," "Hidden: The Secret Jews of Spain," "Whisper Freedom: The Soviet Jewry Struggle" (with Sharon Katz), and "David, the Servant King" (with Shlomit Koffler Weinreb). Avital has also been creating an album of songs inspired by biblical characters, giving voice to the hopes, struggles, and dreams of figures we thought we knew. Her songs can be enjoyed at www.youtube.com/@avitalmacales, where the ancient and the contemporary meet in harmony.

Briana Grogin grew up in Los Angeles in a warm and loving family. A graduate of UCLA, she married Eli Grogin, in 2006, and a week later they made aliyah. They currently live in a yishuv in the center of the country with their children. Briana works as a therapist for women and girls.

Dr. Chana Tannenbaum has been a sought-after Jewish educator for over 30 years. She was the recipient of the Baumel Award as the most outstanding faculty member at Yeshiva University, where she taught and earned her doctorate in Jewish Education and Administration. Since making aliyah with her family in 1997 to Nof Ayalon, she has taught Tanach and Education in Bar Ilan University, Michlelet Herzog, and Matan. Dr. Tannenbaum's new book, *Conceived in Hope: The Struggles of Biblical Mothers in the Tapestry of Redemption*, is available from Koren and via Amazon.

Dina Guedalia is a certified Qi Gong and Tai Chi instructor, and a Total

Wellness coach. Previously, she worked in research of genetic disease at Shaare Zedek Medical Center. She received her BA in biology from Bar-Ilan University and her masters in Biotech from Hebrew University. Recently, she trained at the Binu college in Jerusalem. The program enables one to gradually learn to reframe and create a mindset that is redemptive through a unique blend of Torah, psychology, trauma release techniques, and more. Dina, a mother of seven, lives in Beit Shemesh with her husband, David. Their son, Yosef Malachi, was killed in battle while protecting the people and the land on October 7th. https://sites. google.com/view/yosefmalachiguedalia/home

Rabbanit Etta Bendavid is a licensed pastoral counselor in private practice, specializing in loss and grief, and a qualified *morah l'halachah*. Etta earned MA degrees in Midrash/Theology and Education and has been teaching for many years, incorporating her passion for music and drama. Together with her husband, Rav Eitan Bendavid, Etta made aliyah in 2017 to Ra'anana, where she serves as rabbanit at Kehillat Shivtei Yisrael in Raanana and is proud mother to Aryeh Lev, Boaz, Talya and Adir. She leads a musical Hallel for women nearly every Rosh Chodesh. Find her at SpiritualCareIsrael.com

Hila Bar hails from Cape Town, South Africa, and currently lives in the Emek HaElah region of Israel. Hila is a professional translator and editor, as well as a writer of poetry and prose. Her themes primarily include the exploration of her deep-set inner feelings and pain, and her observation of the outside world, which ranges from societal behavior and vast landscapes to a crawling ant or a broken chair on the side of the road. She is presently working on her first novel. Hila is also the founder of Iron Words Israel, an arts and literature website that showcases people's creative written submissions about the Israel-Hamas war; musical and art submissions are welcome, too: www.ironwordsisrael.com

Jessica Levine Kupferberg made aliyah with her family from La Jolla, California in 2014. A former attorney, she is a writer, poet, and blogger whose work has been featured in numerous publications, including *The Jerusalem Post, The Times of Israel, Jewish Journal,* and *The Jewish Press,* as well as anthologies about the pandemic and life after October 7th. She is a proud wife, mother and "Savti" who loves reading, food, and travel, and is always grateful to come home.

Dr. Juliana (Joolz) Brown is a translator and editor. A mother of five, she lives in Pardes Hanna-Karkur, and has spent the past five years driving her soldier-daughters to and from the train station.

Rabbanit Karen Miller Jackson is a certified *meshivat Halacha,* Jewish educator, and writer known for her contributions to Torah studies and educational initiatives, including at the Matan Institute for Torah Studies. She is a member of the second cohort of Sacks Scholars. Karen is writing a book on Aggadah in Talmud Berakhot, is the creator of #PowerParsha, hosts the Eden Center podcast, "Women & Wellbeing," and is the founder of Kivun l'Sherut, a guidance program for religious girls before *sherut le'umi* or army service. Karen has an MA in Talmud and Midrash from NYU. She lives with her family in Ra'anana, Israel.

Michal Porat Zibman teaches at Midreshet Moriah and Machon Maayan, and regularly guides both student and adult groups on journeys to Poland. She spends her summers as a division head at Camp HASC, a seven-week overnight camp for children and adults with specialized needs. She lives in Neve Daniel with her husband and three children

Rachel Berko is author of the recently published book, *Infinite Potential: A Journey of the Soul through Poetry and Prayer,* (Mosaica Press). Rachel grew up in New York and currently lives in *Eretz Yisrael* with her husband and children.

Rachel Weinstein is a social worker in private practice who helps teens and adults facing grief, adjustment, and trauma, and is passionate about working with LGBTQ individuals and their families, particularly within the Orthodox and greater Jewish community. Rachel believes that everyone has a story that deserves to be heard and is grateful to those who entrust her with theirs. Rachel and her family live in Israel. Find her at www.rachelweinsteinmsw.com and IG: @rachelweinsteinmsw

After serving in the US military, **Ruti Eastman** married her hero, discovered Judaism, and homeschooled four sons. She and her family made aliyah in 2007. Ruti's articles and poetry have been published in a number of online journals. Ruti is the author of two books of short essays and two books of poetry, largely devoted to her aliyah experience. She enjoys playing harmonica and percussion with her family band. Ruti lives with her husband in Neve Daniel in Gush Etzion.

Sarah Ansbacher is a writer and novelist. She was born in the UK and now lives in Modiin. Her latest book, *Wave after Wave*, is a historical novel based on a true story about a group of Jewish refugees from Nazi-occupied Europe who make a clandestine immigration attempt to Eretz Israel/ British-controlled Mandatory Palestine during World War II. Her previous books include the novel, *Ayuni*, and *Passage from Aden*, a collection of short stories based on her experiences working in the Aden Jewish Heritage Museum in Tel Aviv. Find her at: https://www.sarah-ansbacher.com/; https://www.facebook.com/SarahAnsbacherAuthor; and IG: https://www.instagram.com/sarahansbacherwrites

Sarah Sassoon is an Australian born, Iraqi Jewish writer, poet, and educator. She is the author of the award winning picture book, *Shoham's Bangle* and *This is Not a Cholent*, as well as the award-winning online poetry micro-chapbook, *This Is Why We Don't Look* (Harbor Review). She lives in Jerusalem with her husband and four boys. For more of her writing, visit www.sarahsassoon.com

Sarah Tuttle-Singer author of *Jerusalem Drawn and Quartered* and the New Media Editor at *The Times of Israel*, was raised in Venice Beach, CA, on Yiddish lullabies and civil rights anthems. Now living in Jerusalem with her three kids, she explores the city's hidden corners and secret doors and writes about its people.

Senai Guedalia made aliyah to Jerusalem and married Yosef Hy"d a year before October 7. Yosef fell on Simchat Torah, protecting civilians and soldiers in Kfar Aza. Senai lives her life because of, alongside, and for Yosef, and tries to share more and more of his light every day.

Sherri Mandell received a National Jewish Book Award in 2004 for her spiritual memoir, *The Blessing of a Broken Heart,* which was translated into three languages and produced as a play in Jerusalem and the US. Her latest book is *The Kabbalah of Writing: Mystical Practices for Inspiration and Creativity.* She is also the author of *Reaching for Comfort: What I Saw, What I Learned and How I Blew It Training as a Pastoral Counselor; The Road to Resilience: From Chaos to Celebration; Writers of the Holocaust;* and two children's picture books, *The Elephant in the Sukkah* and *The Upside-Down Boy and the Israeli Prime Minister.*

Shoshana Judelman teaches Chasidus in the Shirat David Community in Efrat and at Midreshet Rachel V'Chaya Women's Institute in Jerusalem. Shoshana also leads inspirational trips to Poland and Ukraine as well as around Israel. She holds a masters in Jewish history and has been a guide at Yad Vashem since 2014.

Sorelle Weinstein, a former book editor turned health and weight loss coach, helps others transform their lives through mindset and wellness. Originally from Manchester, England, she made aliyah at 20, and lives in Rehovot with her husband, three daughters, and their Golden Retriever, Cadbury — named after her favorite chocolate.

Tamar Ron Marvin is a graduate of Yeshivat Maharat and holds a PhD in medieval and early modern Jewish Studies. She is at work on her first book, an intellectual history of the era of the *Rishonim*, and lives in Modiin with her family.

Talia (Friedman) Haber was born in Teaneck, NJ. After college, she made aliyah, and, shortly thereafter, met and married her husband. They had three children together. On January 16, 2024, Hamas killed her loving husband, Zechariah Haber, who was serving in the IDF reserves. Find her at: https://www.facebook.com/talia.friedman.9/

Toby Klein Greenwald is an award-winning journalist and theater director, a poet, playwright and co-founder and editor-in-chief of WholeFamily.com. Her theater projects include Raise Your Spirits Theatre, "Mikva the Musical, Music & Monologues from the Deep" and the Na'na and

Hamra Playback Troupes. She is the recipient of the Life Achievement Award from ATARA, The Association for Torah and the Arts. She has taught Torah, Jewish Thought, Theater, English, and Creative Writing and has degrees from Jerusalem College for Women, Hebrew University, and an MA from Bar-Ilan University. She is the translator of the book, *In the Land of Prayer, Personal Tefillot from Israel in Turbulent Times*, and was the initiator, interviewer and first editor of Rabbi Shlomo Riskin's memoir, *Listening to God: Inspirational Stories for My Grandchildren*. Find her at: https://www.linkedin.com/in/toby-klein-greenwald-bb10103/

Tzipora Lifchitz is a creator, writer, and photographer, who captures the essence of life in Israel. Her writing navigates the challenges of conflict, the importance of staying centered in difficult times, and the realities of raising children during war. She views creativity as a powerful tool for fostering hope and building connections. Tzipora lives in Jerusalem with her husband and their five children.

After an adventurous and unattributable career in security and intelligence, **Yael Shahar** now divides her time between writing about Jewish philosophy and learning Talmud with anyone who will sit still long enough. She is the author of *Returning*, a remarkable true story of spiritual resilience. A dynamic and sought-after public speaker, Yael has lectured worldwide on topics ranging from counterterrorism to Gemara. Her writing on Jewish history and philosophy can be found at www.yaelshahar.com.

Dr. Yael Levine holds a PhD in Talmud from Bar-Ilan University. She has published numerous studies, mainly focusing on issues related to women and Judaism. She has also composed many prayers and midrashim.

Yael Sukenik was born in New England, raised in Atlanta, and made aliyah in 2002. Yael is a writer with a love of liturgy and an interest in comparative *nuschaot* and other Jewish cultural intersections, as well as parenting through a lens of transmitting culture and values. She currently lives in Jerusalem with her husband and two boys, who aspire to add a dog to the picture.

Yael Unterman is a Jerusalem-based author. Her two books are *Nehama Leibowitz: Teacher and Bible Scholar* (National Jewish Book Award finalist, 2009) and *The Hidden of Things: Twelve Stories of Love & Longing* (USA Best Book Awards finalist, 2015). She is a lecturer at Shalem College and worldwide, and has conducted more than 750 Torah study workshops using the Bibliodrama method.

Artists

Avigail Wieder is an artist and inspirer living in Jerusalem creating artwork that lights up one's soul and lights up one's life. Originally from London, she spent way too much time pursuing all things besides art, instead of doing the thing she does best. Thank God, she now paints full time, creating masterpieces for collectors across the world, selling through galleries and her online shop, and sharing her inspiration and stories on social media. When not painting, she is hanging with her husband and kids, or walking Jerusalem streets and hills dreaming up the next creations. www.avigailwieder.com

Avital Sharansky was born in the former Soviet Union and was deeply moved by Israel's light when she made aliyah in 1974. She lives and paints in Jerusalem, where she enjoys the company of her husband, daughters, sons-in-law, and grandchildren, and continues to explore the light of the land of Israel.

Bracha Lankin is an artist based in Jerusalem, where creativity has been a lifelong thread woven into every stage of life. A mom of two, she finds inspiration in everyday moments, shaping stories through art and connection. While she now curates artistic experiences through her event production company, her work remains rooted in a deep love for creativity and expression. Find her at https://www.blstudio.org/

Inbal Singer is a bilingual, proud Israeli-American artist living in sunny Beit Shemesh. Her art conveys themes of healing, growth and inspiration through natural elements. Find her at: Instagram @hummingbirddesignprints and https://israelfineart.com/collections/inbal-singer

Leah Jacobson is both an artist and a Jewish educator, drawing inspiration from the beauty and wonder of God's world. Her distinctive style blends art with deep Torah themes, creating pieces that are both meaningful and visually striking. By incorporating a variety of materials — including found objects — each work remains truly one-of-a-kind. https://leahj19.wixsite.com/leahjart

Leah Luria, a mother of seven and a classically trained fine artist, made aliyah with her family in 2021 from South Florida. Since making aliyah, Leah's work has focused on the vibrant colors and spirituality of Israel, inviting viewers to journey through Israel's breathtaking rolling hills and sacred landscapes. Shortly after October 7th, Leah founded IsraelFineArt.com, initially as a collaborative fundraiser for widows and orphans in Israel, which evolved into an online gallery/shop. IsraelFineArt.com aims to help showcase artists in Israel, offering a range of styles of beautiful artwork as fine art prints and gifts, contemporary kitchenware, colorful accessories, and unique home decor.

Micol Bayer is a papercut artist who works closely with her clients to bring beauty and meaning into her creations. She is drawn to the balance of positive and negative space that create the elegance of a papercut, and is inspired by the natural beauty of the land of Israel. Her papercutting style and motifs are constantly evolving.

Ronit Friedman is an American-Israeli artist who brings the land of Israel to life with rich colors and loose brushstrokes. Her original acrylic paintings capture the beauty of Jerusalem and the Israeli landscape. Ronit's paintings have been exhibited in Israel and internationally. Her work is available for purchase at www.ronitfriedman.com

Sefira Lightstone is a Jerusalem-based illustrator and activist whose art empowers Jews to connect with their heritage. Her work has been featured by major Jewish organizations, including Chabad.org and *The Forward*. With a unique style that blends tradition and modernity, Sefira uses her creativity to challenge stereotypes and inspire others. In addition to her professional work, she is a mother, runner, and coffee-lover . Find her work at sefiracreative.com and follow her on IG at SefiraCreative.

Renowned glass blower and painter **Sheva Chaya Shaiman** is a Princeton graduate who made aliyah to Tzfat in 1997. She enriches her popular gallery in the Artists' Quarter by sharing her journey and unique artistic insights with thousands of visitors annually. Sheva Chaya teaches painting, glassblowing, and Torah and art workshops, and also offers transformative Yoga classes that deepen the mind-body-soul connection.

American-Israeli **Yael Harris Resnick** is a self-taught multimedia artist known for her hand-painted silk, acrylic paintings and, most strikingly, integrating silk accents on her canvases. Influenced by her mother, calligrapher and ketubah artist Hedy Harris, much of Yael's work involves Judaic and biblical motifs and illustrates the splendor of the land of Israel using a vibrantly colorful palette. Inspired by great female artists like Freda Khalo, Yael strives to bring brave female heroines into the limelight. She is an award-winning artist who has been recognized by the Washington, DC Calligraphers Guild, Israel's Artists Guild, and Israel's Ministry of Industry, Trade and Labor. She lives in Israel with her husband and four kids. You can find her work at https://yaelharris-resnick.com/

The Az Nashir Series

by The SHVILLI Center & The Layers Press

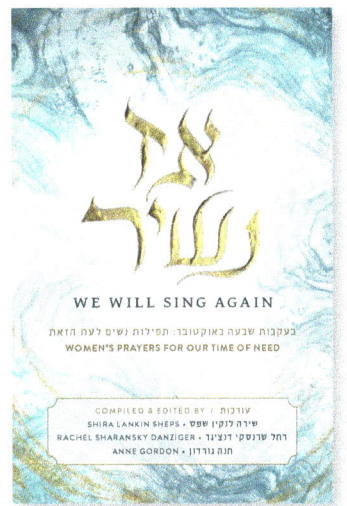 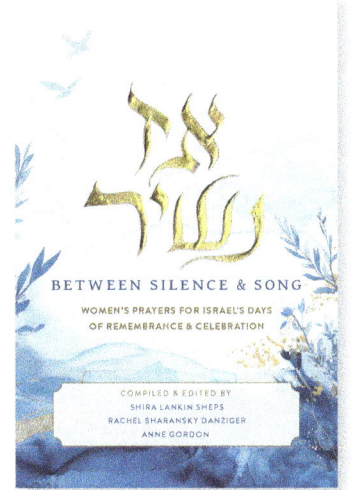

Available at www.shvillicenter.org and on Amazon.

Contact us for press and events
at shiralsheps@shvillicenter.org

Follow us on Facebook & Instagram.

Visit our website at

www.shvillicenter.org

to learn about the writing workshops we offer
and check out our guide
to writing your own *tefillot* and *techinot*.

www.ingramcontent.com/pod-product-compliance
Lightning Source LLC
Chambersburg PA
CBHW051310120626
46547CB00015B/2177